Technology Timesavers:
Simple Steps to Increasing Classroom Productivity

Mary Ploski Seamon

Eric J. Levitt

Library of Congress Cataloging-in-Publication Data

Seamon, Mary Ploski, 1943-
   Technology timesavers: simple steps to increasing classroom productivity / Mary Ploski Seamon and Eric J. Levitt.
      p. cm.
   Includes bibliographical references and index.
   ISBN 1-58683-122-4
    1. Computer-assisted instruction. 2. Internet in education. 3. Effective teaching. I. Levitt, Eric J., 1970- II. Title.

LB1028.5.S378 2003
371-33 '4--dc21

2003043571

Published by Linworth Publishing, Inc.
480 East Wilson Bridge Road, Suite L
Worthington, Ohio 43085

Copyright © 2003 by Linworth Publishing, Inc.

All rights reserved. Purchasing this book entitles a librarian to reproduce activity sheets for use in the library within a school or entitles a teacher to reproduce activity sheets for single classroom use within a school. Other portions of the book (up to 15 pages) may be copied for staff development purposes within a single school. Standard citation information should appear on each page. The reproduction of any part of this book for an entire school or school system or for commercial use is strictly prohibited. No part of this book may be electronically reproduced, transmitted, or recorded without written permission from the publisher.

ISBN: 1-58683-122-4

5 4 3 2 1

Table of Contents

List of Figures vii

Acknowledgements xi

Introduction I Don't Have Time To Think 1

Chapter 1 **Saving Time** 5
- Time to Plan 5
- Changing the Classroom 5
- Maintaining a Focus on Student Achievement 6
- Changes in a Teacher's Role 7
- Simple Steps 8
- The Exhibit Center 10
- Show Me How It's Done 10
- The Disappearing URL 10

Chapter 2 **Organize It: Managing Bookmarks** 11
- I Have Too Much to Do 11
- Heartaches and Frustrations 12
- New Timesaving Features 12
- Improving Technology-Based Instruction with Bookmarks and Tabs ... 12
- **Exhibit Center** 14
  - Bookmarking with Internet Explorer 14
  - Bookmarking with Netscape 16
  - Web-Based Bookmark Management 17
  - Tabs: A New Look at Bookmarking 18
  - Saving Favorites to a Floppy Disk 19
- **Show Me How It's Done** 20
  - Creating Bookmarks with Internet Explorer 20
  - Creating Bookmarks with Netscape 22
  - Using Backflip to Manage Bookmarks Online 24
  - Using iKeepBookmarks to Manage Favorites Online ... 27
  - Creating Tab Groups with CrystalPort Web Browser ... 29
  - Creating Saved Window Setups with Opera Web Browser ... 31

Chapter 3 **Thinking with Bubbles** 33
- Why Use Inspiration? 33
- Clarify Thinking 34
- Sample Applications 35
- Background Using Inspiration 39
- **Exhibit Center** 40
  - Examples of Inspiration as a Classroom Tool 40
- **Show Me How It's Done** 43
  - What Is Inspiration? 43

	Getting Started	43
	Adding Text to a Symbol	44
	Insert a New Symbol	45
	Linking Symbols	45
	Using RapidFire	46
	Changing Symbol's Appearance	47
	Opening a Template	49
	Saving a Custom Template	50
	Notes on Using Kidspiration	51
	Getting Started with a Kidspiration Diagram	51
	Examples Using Kidspiration	52
Chapter 4	**Assessment Tools to Improve Classroom Instruction**	**55**
	So What Do We Know?	56
	How Can We Do It?	56
	Hot Potatoes	56
	The Six Applications	57
	Applications Are Easy to Use	59
	Strengths of Hot Potatoes	59
	Exhibit Center	**60**
	Examples of Assessment Materials on the Web	60
	Other Interactive Exercise Makers	64
	Interactive Exercise Makers	65
	Show Me How It's Done	**67**
	Getting Started	67
	Using Hot Potatoes to Create Quizzes	70
	First Steps—Starting Hot Potatoes	71
	Using JBC	72
	Steps to Creating an Exercise	72
	Adding Text	73
	Adding Reading Text	73
	Inserting a Picture	74
	Saving Your Files	75
	Using JQuiz	76
	Using JMix	77
	Using JCross	78
	Using JMatch	79
	Using JCloze	79
Chapter 5	**Worksheet Wonders and More**	**81**
	What Do Students Know?	81
	Why Use Worksheets?	81
	When Is the Use of a Worksheet Appropriate?	82
	Enhancing Instruction	82
	Worksheet Generator	83
	PuzzleMaker	84
	Web Tools for Educators	85

    Bingo Maker 85
    Personal Educational Press 86
    The Learning Page. 86
    SuperKids Math Worksheet Generator 87
    A+ Math. 87
    Exhibit Center 88
        Elements of the Periodic Table: Word Scramble. 88
        Elements of the Periodic Table: Matching Quiz 89
    Show Me How It's Done 94
        Using Worksheet Generator. 94
        Saving Your Worksheet 95
        Creating a Worksheet Using PuzzleMaker Vocabulary Lists 96
        One Click Does It 97
        Creating Other Mazes 97
        Creating Other Puzzles 98
        Copying or Printing Your Puzzle. 98
        Personal Educational Press 99
        Creating Flash Cards. 100

Chapter 6 Making the Grade 101
    Why Assess? 101
    Grades Are Important 101
    Teaching to the Test 102
    Using Rubrics to Define Instruction 102
    Three Tools to Develop Rubrics 103
    RubiStar. 103
    ClassWeb 104
    Teacher Rubric Generator 105
    Exhibit Center 106
        Rubric on Edgar Allan Poe Report 106
        WebQuest Evaluation Form. 107
        Persuasive Essay Rubric 108
    Show Me How It's Done 109
        Using RubiStar 109
        Using ClassWeb Rubric Builder 112
        Performance Indicators 113
        Rubric Generator. 116

Chapter 7 Search It! Using Search Engines Effectively . . . 119
    Seek and Ye Shall Find . . . Sometimes. 119
    Why Use Search Engines 120
    There Is a Better Way 120
    Comparison of Search Engines/Directories. 121
    Did You Say Google?. 121
    Exhibit Center 122
        The Google Interface. 122
        Google Snapshots 122
        I'm Feeling Lucky. 124

		Safe Search Filtering	125
		Google's Advanced Features	125
		The Google Toolbar	127
	Show Me How It's Done		130
		The Search Is On	130

Chapter 8 What's Next? 135
    Struggling to Stay Above Water 135
    Making the Whole Bigger than Its Parts 135
    The Same Way of Thinking 136
    Misguided Effort 136
    Taming the Technology 136
    Energize, Refresh, and Renew 137
    Competent and Committed Teachers 137

Appendix: Source List 139

Index 141

About the Authors 147

List of Figures

Figure 1.1	Bloom's Taxonomy	7
Figure 2.1	Favorites Menu	14
Figure 2.2	Favorites Button	14
Figure 2.3	Looking in a Folder	15
Figure 2.4	Expanding a Folder	15
Figure 2.5	The Netscape Bookmarks Menu	16
Figure 2.6	Netscape Sidebar	16
Figure 2.7	Backflipping Bookmarks	17
Figure 2.8	Bookmarking with iKeepBookmarks	17
Figure 2.9	Bookmarking with MyBookmarks	18
Figure 2.10	CrystalPort Browser Tab Group	18
Figure 2.11	Tiled Windows in Opera Software Web Browser	19
Figure 2.12	Favorites Button	20
Figure 2.13	Favorites Window	21
Figure 2.14	Adding a Favorite	21
Figure 2.15	Adding a Folder to Favorites	22
Figure 2.16	Bookmarks Menu	22
Figure 2.17	Add Bookmark Window	23
Figure 2.18	Adding a Folder to Bookmarks	23
Figure 2.19	Backflip Login	24
Figure 2.20	Backflip Navigation Menu	25
Figure 2.21	My Folders in Backflip	25
Figure 2.22	Backflip Management Menu	26
Figure 2.23	Creating a New Folder in Backflip	26
Figure 2.24	Adding a Bookmark to Backflip	27
Figure 2.25	Bookmarks in iKeepBookmarks	28
Figure 2.26	Adding a New Folder Button	28
Figure 2.27	Adding a New Folder Screen	28
Figure 2.28	Adding a New Bookmark Button	29
Figure 2.29	Adding a New Bookmark to iKeepBookmarks	29
Figure 2.30	Adding a Tab from Favorites	30
Figure 2.31	Tab Toolbar	30
Figure 2.32	Viewing Tabs in Tile Mode	30
Figure 2.33	Window Bar and Creating Linked Windows	31
Figure 2.34	Windows Tiled in Opera Web Browser	32
Figure 3.1	Brace Map	35
Figure 3.2	Double Bubble Map	36
Figure 3.3	Thinking-Idea Map Template	36
Figure 3.4	Brainstorming the Causes of the American Civil War	37
Figure 3.5	Template to Organize Knowledge on the Civil War	37
Figure 3.6	Causes and Impact of the American Civil War	38
Figure 3.7	Brainstorming Results of Harvesting of the Rain Forest	40

Figure 3.8	Exploring Impact of Deforestation	40
Figure 3.9	Brainstorming Basic Needs of Animals Unit	41
Figure 3.10	Animal Survival Guided Tour	41
Figure 3.11	Brainstorming Animal Survival Needs	42
Figure 3.12	Brainstorming Causes of Weather	42
Figure 3.13	Inspiration Screen	44
Figure 3.14	Main Idea	44
Figure 3.15	Continents	45
Figure 3.16	Adding Ideas	45
Figure 3.17	Link	46
Figure 3.18	Creating a Link	46
Figure 3.19	RapidFire	46
Figure 3.20	Using RapidFire	47
Figure 3.21	RapidFire Diagram	47
Figure 3.22	Symbol Palette	48
Figure 3.23	Using Graphics	48
Figure 3.24	Opening a Template	49
Figure 3.25	Selecting a Template	49
Figure 3.26	Saving a Diagram as a Template	50
Figure 3.27	Kidspiration Opening Screen	51
Figure 3.28	Kidspiration Screen	51
Figure 3.29	The Listen Button	52
Figure 3.30	Characteristics of a Rabbit	52
Figure 3.31	A Profile of China	53
Figure 3.32	An Aquarium Ecosystem	53
Figure 4.1	Crossword Puzzle	57
Figure 4.2	Multiple-Choice Quiz	58
Figure 4.3	Lab Equipment	58
Figure 4.4	Review of Poetry Terms	60
Figure 4.5	A Journey Through Poe	60
Figure 4.6	Poe's "Annabel Lee"	61
Figure 4.7	Poe's Biographical Information	61
Figure 4.8	American Writers	62
Figure 4.9	The "I Have A Dream Speech"	62
Figure 4.10	American Writers—Matching	62
Figure 4.11	American Writers Series	63
Figure 4.12	Mixed-Up Sentence	63
Figure 4.13	WebPractest Exercise	64
Figure 4.14	Interactive Exercise Maker at Swarthmore College	65
Figure 4.15	Example of Clozemaker	66
Figure 4.16	Example of EvalMaker	66
Figure 4.17	Example of MatchMaker	66
Figure 4.18	Example of MultiMaker	66
Figure 4.19	Hot Potatoes Homepage	67
Figure 4.20	Downloads	67
Figure 4.21	File Download	68
Figure 4.22	Save As	68

Figure 4.23	Desktop	69
Figure 4.24	Self-Extractor	69
Figure 4.25	Setup	69
Figure 4.26	Setup Wizard	70
Figure 4.27	Hot Potatoes Short Cut	71
Figure 4.28	Click on Potato	71
Figure 4.29	JBC Screen	72
Figure 4.30	Add Text	73
Figure 4.31	Dialogue Box	73
Figure 4.32	Insert Picture	74
Figure 4.33	Saving Files	74
Figure 4.34	Information Box	75
Figure 4.35	Web Page File	75
Figure 4.36	JQuiz	76
Figure 4.37	American Literature Example	76
Figure 4.38	JMix	77
Figure 4.39	JMix Example	77
Figure 4.40	JCross	78
Figure 4.41	Crossword Grid	78
Figure 4.42	Adding Clues	78
Figure 4.43	JMatch	79
Figure 4.44	JCloze	79
Figure 4.45	Creating a Gap	80
Figure 4.46	Gapped Words Alternative	80
Figure 5.1	Worksheet Generator	83
Figure 5.2	Ready-To-Go Worksheets	84
Figure 5.3	PuzzleMaker Examples	84
Figure 5.4	Entering Words in a Grid	85
Figure 5.5	Bingo Maker Generator	85
Figure 5.6	Selecting Word Lists	86
Figure 5.7	Sample Quiz from Personal Education Press	90
Figure 5.8	Sample Flash Cards (Front) from Personal Education Press	91
Figure 5.9	Sample Flash Cards (Back) from Personal Education Press	92
Figure 5.10	Sample Bingo Board from Personal Education Press	93
Figure 5.11	Discovery School's Worksheet Generator	94
Figure 5.12	Create a Worksheet	94
Figure 5.13	Print Your Worksheet	95
Figure 5.14	Options for Saving Your Worksheet	96
Figure 5.15	Create a Matching Quiz Using Word Lists	96
Figure 5.16	Cool Mazes	97
Figure 5.17	Animal Maze Collection	97
Figure 5.18	Advanced Maze Creation	98
Figure 5.19	Create Puzzles Online	98
Figure 5.20	Selecting the Output Style	99
Figure 5.21	Vocabulary Lists and Answer Lists	99
Figure 5.22	Study Sheet Options	100
Figure 5.23	Flash Card Selection	100

Figure 6.1	Sample Topics on RubiStar	104
Figure 6.2	ClassWeb Rubric Builder	105
Figure 6.3	Rubric Samples from Rubric Generator	105
Figure 6.4	RubiStar	109
Figure 6.5	Rubric Samples	109
Figure 6.6	Multimedia Project Rubric	110
Figure 6.7	Rating Scale	110
Figure 6.8	Making Your Category Selections	111
Figure 6.9	Rating Scale Criteria	111
Figure 6.10	Printing or Saving the Rubric	111
Figure 6.11	Tutorials	112
Figure 6.12	Completed Rubric	112
Figure 6.13	Rubric Builder Start Page	113
Figure 6.14	Building a Rubric with ClassWeb Rubric Builder	113
Figure 6.15	Completed Objectives	114
Figure 6.16	Completing Your Rubric	114
Figure 6.17	A Saved Rubric	115
Figure 6.18	HTML Code	115
Figure 6.19	Persuasive Essay Rubric	115
Figure 6.20	Calculating Score	116
Figure 6.21	Rubric Generator	116
Figure 6.22	Insert a Picture	117
Figure 6.23	Paragraph Writing Rubric	117
Figure 7.1	Google Home Page	122
Figure 7.2	Hits Returned by Google	123
Figure 7.3	Cached Web Site	123
Figure 7.4	Poe Hit List	124
Figure 7.5	I'm Feeling Lucky	124
Figure 7.6	Filtering Options	125
Figure 7.7	Google Advanced Search Page	125
Figure 7.8	Find Results	126
Figure 7.9	Language Search	126
Figure 7.10	Date Search	126
Figure 7.11	Occurrences Search	127
Figure 7.12	News Search	127
Figure 7.13	Google Toolbar Link	128
Figure 7.14	System Requirements and Language Selection	128
Figure 7.15	Install the Google Toolbar	129
Figure 7.16	The Google Toolbar	129
Figure 7.17	Searching With All of the Words	130
Figure 7.18	Google Inserts Quotation Operator	131
Figure 7.19	Syntax for at Least One of the Words	131
Figure 7.20	Without the Words Field	131
Figure 7.21	File Format Search Field	132
Figure 7.22	Occurrences Field	132
Figure 7.23	Domain Search	133

Acknowledgements

We have the good fortune of working with wonderful people who care about others. From the superintendent, Dr. Jim Ray, and the Spartanburg School District 3 Board of Trustees, to the teachers and media specialists who are enthusiastic about teaching and learning, and especially to the students and parents who support the district, we thank you.

We would like to thank Donnie Elder and Sherri Horton. Donnie is the wonderful technology coordinator for Spartanburg School District 3 who keeps everything running in top shape—with good humor no less. Sherri has the dubious distinction of being everything to everyone. As administrative assistant to Mary and Donnie, she goes beyond the call of duty on every task.

We would also like to thank our families. To Carmen, Eric's wife, and their daughter Grace, warm kisses and hugs. To Mary's children—Trevor, Soc, and Kathy (Soc's wonderful wife)—heartfelt hugs and kisses and thanks for patient encouragement.

Introduction

I Don't Have Time to Think

> *"Time is a great teacher, but unfortunately it kills all its pupils"*
>
> —*Hector Louis Berlioz*

Our first book, *Web-based Learning: A Practical Guide* (Linworth, 2001), discussed how to create Web-based lessons that evolved into the richness and complexity of well-designed WebQuests. *Web-based Learning: A Practical Guide* contains wonderful examples of teachers aligning activities to the academic content standards and developing innovative lesson plans that involve experiential learning for students through the use of local resources and primary documents.

As training in the *Web-based Learning* model continues, it seems that the process of acquiring and becoming proficient in some of the more basic technology skills has created some of the largest problems.

Beginning with Hotlists (a list of Web sites collected around a topic), groans and cries of frustration would sound out over missing lists of Internet favorites. Or, inevitably, as each of us has said at one point, *"They're gone, just gone!"*

And one of the most common refrains uttered, *"I know a wonderful site. It would be perfect! How do I find it again?"*

Another valid concern often expressed, *"How are students going to access these sites in one class period? It'll take them that long to click on all of the links."*

These dilemmas made us re-examine our approach. After all, it is all of us in education who must meet the ever-growing demands of diverse populations of parents and students as well as the intensifying scrutiny of public opinion. With twice as much to teach, and twice as much testing of what is taught, teachers need to save time. This book does not try to solve these bigger problems, but it does offer many useful timesaving tips that benefit all of us in education.

The question then became what timesaving tips are most important? Out of the hundreds and hundreds of timesaving tips available through the Web and other technology, which tips would have the most impact in assisting teachers as they develop project-based Web lessons?

Reflecting on the many hours of training sessions and conversations with teachers, the key ideas on which to focus became quite clear. Teachers in the field know exactly which things are needed in order to develop their lessons most appropriately.

Here is what the professionals had to say:

1. Provide steps to organize materials already acquired.
2. Provide support and examples toward generating ideas and in mapping those ideas into a useable project.
3. Point out some quick assessment techniques that will not require additional hours grading papers.
4. Demonstrate how to vary assessments so they can be fun.
5. Offer assistance in developing materials to reinforce what needs to be learned.
6. Give guidance in developing rubrics. How do we assess student projects? How can we assess a student presentation?
7. Identify some good search techniques on the Web that will save time.
8. Help find varied resources to build relevant lessons.

We all are usually excited about developing projects but are sometimes slowed by the necessity of coming up with a project topic. Or, a topic may present itself quickly, but developing it fully can be awfully time-consuming. We all try to minimize the likelihood of spending hours developing ideas that prove to be a dead-end. How do we prevent this from happening; what can we do differently?

At times, contradictions were unavoidable. How do you reconcile a pen-and-pencil test for an engaging, inquiry-based lesson? It just doesn't seem to fit.

Some other insightful questions include:

"This is all well and good, but how am I suppose to grade it?"
"How do you grade group work?"
"How can you distinguish between an 'A' PowerPoint presentation and a 'B' PowerPoint presentation?"

One of the biggest challenges for any type of trainer is avoiding the assumption of knowledge. Our natural tendency is to assume that everyone knows everything that we know. Combating these assumptions is a hallmark of an effective trainer.

Usually technology classes begin with the media specialist or technology trainer surveying teachers about their experiences in using the Web. While several years ago it was very common to find people with little experience using the Web, most teachers now enter the technology class professing to be very knowledgeable. They have used the Web to find lessons and to research information. The chief concern now appears to be that *"It's too time-consuming to use the Web."*

Exploring this concern more thoroughly usually leads to the finding that although teachers have been using the Web, they use it by going to sites recommended in books or by their peers. In other words, many teachers—even those who are most knowledgeable—have not learned to search the Web efficiently. This problem, as any media specialists can attest, is not a teacher problem only—many students who are techno whizzes have not learned to search either.

Still, at other training sessions, a recurring sentiment voiced is not being able to find anything on the Web that really relates to a particular lesson or unit.

"This may be all well and good for teachers studying dinosaurs with their students, but it certainly does not work for chemistry. I can't waste time."

After listening to the teachers, we decided we needed to write it all down. What better way to process information than to write it?

It seemed to be a natural to put it all in a book. It has become clear that our first book did no go far enough in assisting teachers to use all of the little things that make the Web and other technologies such dynamic parts of the classroom.

Once again, we marvel at the determination, creativity, and resiliency of the classroom teachers that we know. Good teachers know what they want, and they demand it.

We believe that they should get what they want. So once again, this is for those teachers who create those wonderful classrooms—classrooms that are student-focused, high energy, active learning environments.

Chapter 1

Saving Time

> *"Never discourage anyone who continually makes progress, no matter how slow."*
>
> —*Plato*

Schools are part of a larger community. Because of that, we have a great responsibility to communicate clearly to a diverse group of students in order to help them achieve success. Assisting teachers as they raise the achievement of all students by promoting learning that is rooted in relevant experience is the top priority of *Technology Timesavers: Simple Steps to Increasing Classroom Productivity*.

Systemic reform requires changing what we do, why we do it, and how we do it. Although it is well documented that children are more likely to learn if they are able to apply their knowledge, we have made few changes in instructional delivery. We are accustomed to thinking of what is taught in school as information contained in a textbook. This leads to a belief that learning is collecting facts from books and lectures rather than acquiring knowledge through experience and problem solving.

Time to Plan

Without the necessary expertise or *time*, teachers must rely on the textbook. If teachers are to make what is taught in school come alive for students, they must have time to plan, organize, evaluate, and collect information. The wonderful lessons that teachers have identified, refined, disseminated, and published in Web-based applications attest to the talent that teachers have. We hope that we can make a small contribution by suggesting some timesaving tips.

Changing the Classroom

We wonder:
- How can we create classroom contexts and experiences that will enable students to be lifelong learners and problem solvers?

- How can students transfer the knowledge acquired in school to real-life situations?
- How can we engage students in inquiry-based learning?
- How can we serve as a guide for students' inquiries into multiple domains?

Learning is shaped and defined by the context in which it occurs. As our student population has grown more diverse, more is required of us. More visual and kinesthetic than the generations that have gone before, today's students struggle to learn in an auditory environment. Coupling that with the introduction of content standards in the core areas, we realize that students must have a deeper understanding of the subject. Students need to become proficient in ways of applying knowledge that are far more complex than the rote recall of facts and dates.

Remember when it was enough to teach, *"In 1492, Columbus sailed the ocean blue."* (If you recite that ditty in order to figure out when America was discovered, we know your age.)

Or remember the teacher who ensured that we would always spell G-E-O-G-R-A-P-H-Y correctly by teaching us to say, *"George Edens' old granny ran a pig home yesterday."* It's a habit that certainly slows us down as we write geography. (Try to remember how it is spelled, recite the mnemonic device, and type it. Learning is tough stuff.)

It is not that knowledge of when America was discovered or knowledge of how to spell geography correctly is unimportant or wrong. We would hope that all educated folks know that information. However, knowing the facts and dates is not enough in today's society. Things are changing too quickly. We must teach students to problem solve.

The Web is well designed for problem solving. A tremendous variety of materials is available. There are many ideas, and much of the Web's materials are freely shared. Data, newspaper files, opinions, scholarly articles, information Web sites, and more are available.

Most teachers consider using the Web important. They see that the resources and materials that are available on the Web would enhance what they are doing. However, teachers also acknowledge that they simply do not have the time to make good use of those resources.

Maintaining a Focus on Student Achievement

With the passage of the "No Child Left Behind" Act of 2001, we are required to do more, it seems. Maintaining a steadfast focus on student performance in the face of so much high-stakes, large-scale testing is daunting. The pressures are immense. So how do we translate what needs to be taught into engaging and effective classroom experiences for students?

There are some things that keep turning up. In education courses, we were quizzed regularly about Bloom's taxonomy. Well, now is the time to apply that information. With today's standards movement and with the emphasis on critical-thinking skills, Bloom's taxonomy is being resurrected in a big way. It may help to think of learning as moving through all levels of Bloom's taxonomy—knowledge, comprehension, application, analysis, synthesis, and evaluation.

Students have grown accustomed to answering questions at the lower ends of the taxonomy. Teachers check for understanding, for facts, to see if the reading assignment has been read, or to see if the child has followed the story. These are all good techniques and necessary in a classroom. However, if the teacher switches to a higher-level question, the student is lost and confused. What is expected? What are we asking? We can't blame the student for this gap.

We can visualize Bloom's taxonomy as climbing separate ladders that rise higher and higher. If we try to jump up to evaluation without using the other ladders along the way, it is an impossible leap. It requires great courage on the part of student to jump without the safety net of basic information.

If we prepare students by urging them to move comfortably up and down the ladders, they will find it easier to move from one ladder to another ladder or even to jump from one ladder to the other.

Figure 1.1: Bloom's Taxonomy

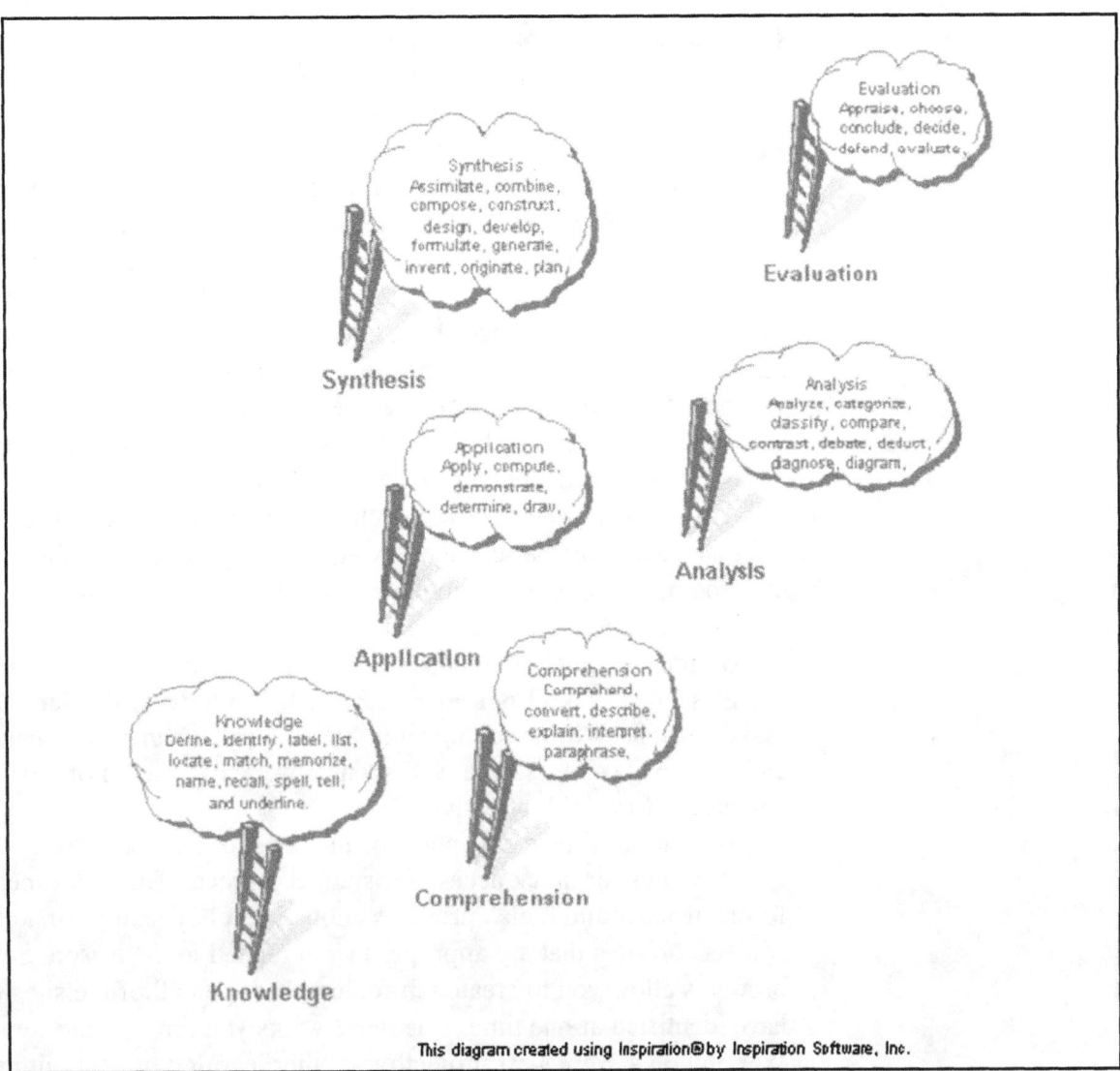

Changes in a Teacher's Role

Computers, distance learning, and other technologies have great potential for supporting changes in a teacher's role. Still, all teachers have to organize material, help students organize the chaos of their thoughts, assess, evaluate, and search for new ideas in every lesson that they create.

As we considered how to make the Web more manageable, we reviewed some common-sense strategies. We organized *Technology Timesavers: Simple Steps to Increasing Classroom Productivity* around these ideas.

Simple Steps

Why did we pick these steps? We wanted to limit the number of steps to the "doable," so that the strategies could be accomplished fairly quickly. We know teachers are busy. The book chapters, therefore, are organized around these crucial steps:

1. **Every lesson needs to be organized.**
   Whether a lesson requires paper copies or pictures, recordings or video, a teacher first needs to know what is available. The same type of organization and preparation must be used with the Web.

   That leads to the first timesaving tip: *Organize it*. Managing bookmarks of useful sites is the first skill that a teacher needs.

   If you can't find it, it won't be of much use. While we may have no trouble imagining someone dumping materials haphazardly into file cabinets, we would all probably agree that the purpose of the file cabinet has been destroyed. Without the simple addition of file folders and tabs, we shouldn't bother with a file cabinet; a box — even a cardboard box — will suffice. It seems that we are far more tolerant of poor organization on the Web than we are with our file cabinets.

   Are we using folders? Do we click **"Add to Favorites"** and have long lists that must be scrolled through? As we move from classroom to classroom, do we lose our bookmarks? Do you have different lists of bookmarks at home and at school?

   Besides the bookmark capability built into most Web browsers, there are sites, such as **MyBookmarks**, **Backflip**, and **iKeepBookmarks**, that make a teacher's life more manageable. Taking the time to manage files and to manage sites is time well spent if we are to use all of the resources of the Web effectively.

   We also must take advantage of the latest trend in browsers, the ability to tab sites for quick access for student projects. This is a timesaver for the teacher and it also provides another level of security in keeping students on sites that are appropriate and related to the lesson. Some browsers allow you to create tab folders that open all of the sites that you have identified at one time. Chapter 2 walks you through the steps. Working on a WebQuest project or another learning project with multiple sites is more manageable when the student can sit at the computer and open all sites referenced at one time.

2. **Students need help in organizing their thinking.**
   For some reason, outlining doesn't work for many people. Most of us will sheepishly acknowledge that when an outline is required, we would first write a draft of the paper and then complete the outline.

With the numerous graphic organizer programs now available, there should be no reason for that to happen again. We have focused on using the software product Inspiration (and Kidspiration) because of the many features available and the simplicity of the interface.

3. **Assessments should be continuous and should help the teacher to refine student learning.**
Engaging and self-paced assessments created through **Hot Potatoes** and other software can be great learning tools for students. Reviewing basic material is essential in building learning. Through repeated assessments, students can review that basic knowledge quickly. Dragging and dropping answers provides the kinesthetic experience that some students need. Quickly creating short-answer quizzes and providing immediate feedback frees the teachers to facilitate more critical learning tasks.

Assessments should be varied and fun. Tests do not have to kill the spirit nor do they have to be a special kind of punishment for the teacher. Long nights of grading tests and quizzes do not have to be the norm.

Students need to know how they are doing and what is expected. They do not necessarily have to be graded, *by the teacher*, on every assignment. Reinforcing learning can be enjoyable. Whether it is the "old trick" of making flash cards or using the knowledge learned by completing a crossword puzzle or a word search, assessments can take varied forms.

4. **Worksheets can be useful in reinforcing learning.**
Giving students the opportunity to take home materials is crucial for home-school relationships. Parents need and want to see what is expected and what is being taught. Generating multiple worksheets on basic learning, such as the periodic table for chemistry, should not be time consuming for the teacher. Using worksheet and quiz generators will save enormous amounts of time for the teacher. Through one list of periodic elements, the teacher can generate multiple exposures to the material.

5. **Students should be informed up-front about how they are being assessed.**
Usually the first question that a student utters after being told that there is a writing assignment or other "subjective" assignment is, *"How are you going to grade it?"* (Were you thinking that the question was going to be, *"How long does it have to be?"*)

Either way, students (and their parents) want to know how their efforts are going to be assessed. If parents or students dispute a grade, having a rubric makes the difference between a teacher having a good day or a bad day. Rubrics state clearly how (and sometimes why) an assignment is judged Superior or Average. It removes the vagueness from grading.

Rubrics also help teachers refine their own thinking about the goals and objectives for the lessons. In this timesaving tip, we focus on building rubrics online. We focus on three rubric builders—**Rubistar**, **ClassWeb Rubric Builder**, and **Rubric Maker**.

6. **Good search techniques can save time.**
   Many teachers do not take the time to learn good search techniques or to familiarize themselves with their Web browsers. While it appears to be time-consuming, learning to search is absolutely essential in using the Web for resource materials. Otherwise, we drift aimlessly around the Web, wondering how time has passed so quickly with so little result.

   Varied resources help build relevant lessons. Computers facilitate teacher inquiry by providing access to vast amounts of information. Through the World Wide Web, teachers can access digital libraries and vast amounts of information in print, visual, and video form. A remarkable example is the American Memory Collection. Through exchange of ideas and resources, quality curriculum and alignment activities that emphasize teacher as facilitator and student as lifelong learner take place.

The Exhibit Center

Within each chapter, we have added an **Exhibit Center**. Designed to save time, the Exhibit Center provides example lessons for classroom use. We think it is important that teachers see what they can create.

We consider the Exhibit Centers as timesavers as well. **If you are a technology trainer or a media specialist who is responsible for technology training, these examples will be of particular value.** Unless we can demonstrate to teachers what we are talking about, it is generally not considered to be important.

Show Me How It's Done

The other critical aspect of each chapter is **Show Me How It's Done**. In a step-by-step format, with liberal use of screen shots, we show you how to recreate what is seen in the Exhibit Center. This too saves time. Instead of searching for a technical manual or searching for instructions in other books or online, the instructions for use are readily available.

During training sessions, the one thing we hear teachers request most often is written directions. During class they may be able to follow along as the media specialists or technology trainer demonstrates, but they find that when they get home, they have forgotten at least one essential step.

The Disappearing URL

Although it is always a risk to put URLs into books—there is always a significant delay between completion and publication—we decided that these sites would survive the delay because of their significance and usefulness. We extend our apologies, in advance, if we are wrong.

Chapter 2

Organize It: Managing Bookmarks

> *"One of the advantages of being disorderly is that one is constantly making exciting discoveries."*
> —*A.A. Milne*

In our jobs, one of the fairly common and most unfortunate scenarios we hear goes something like this, *"I've LOST my favorites!"*

"I spent hours collecting all of those Web sites, and now they are gone."
"Where did my favorites go? Is there any way to retrieve them?"

Or, from those who do not bookmark favorite Web sites, we often hear, *"I came across this great Web site, but I can't remember the address or where I found it."*

I Have Too Much to Do

Of course, at one time or another, everyone is a little, dare we say, *lazy* about saving and organizing important, useful Web sites that took valuable time and effort to locate. Why do we put ourselves through this? Why do we not make the small time investment required to insure that our efforts spent searching for and identifying useful Web sites are not repeated over and over again? Is it that educators are so busy that taking time to bookmark Web sites would just make their work burdens unbearable? Probably not.

More likely, most of us access so much information, so quickly, on the Web that we simply do not take the time to organize the sites that we find into useful, easily accessible bookmarks and folders. Instead, we usually believe that *"I can just visit that Web site again to find the information"* or *"I'll remember where I found that site."*

Heartaches and Frustrations

Even if you are diligent about bookmarking frequently visited Web sites, certain situations still arise that cause heartache and frustration. Many schools and districts place limits on a user's ability to save information, such as bookmarks. Also, often when technology personnel upgrade software or replace aging computers, the bookmarks that we have worked so hard to save, disappear.

Some more advanced technology users know how to export and import their favorites from one Web browser to another, but it is a somewhat confusing and cumbersome process for most of us. So, what's the busy teacher who actually took the time to bookmark to do?

New Timesaving Features

One of the solutions we offer in this chapter is the use of Web-based bookmark management. Often free, these services allow an individual to save bookmarks in a secure account that can be accessed from **any** computer **anywhere** as long as there is an Internet connection.

Another popular trend in the effort to organize our ever-growing collection of Web sites is a feature called *tabs*. Some alternative Web browsers like CrystalPort and Opera allow you to create unique groups of collected Web sites called *tab groups*. This is an enormously useful feature because it enables you to save a group of related Web sites together and afterwards open the entire group in *one* window at the same time. It is nothing to open 10 or 15 sites as a group and simply click from one tab to another to view their contents.

This cool feature not only provides a way to view multiple Web pages at one time but also provides immense value to educators. No matter which way you choose to go, saving and organizing collected Web sites will provide teachers and students more time to make exciting discoveries without the mess.

Improving Technology-Based Instruction with Bookmarks and Tabs

If you are not convinced about the instructional value of bookmarking and tabbing, here is a rundown of some of the immediate advantages of using either or both of these strategies.

- Allows a teacher to structure activities to limit students' access to objectionable sites.
- Expedites the research process if sites are already bookmarked for students.
- Encourages multi-tasking. When creating Web-based activities that require referencing multiple Web pages, teachers can open up entire groups of Web sites, called tabs, and multi-task between them.

- Generates tabs that are very helpful when working with a hotlist of 10 or 20 sites.
- Provides teacher with a very quick overview of which sites are still available. Tabbed groups provide students an opportunity to analyze and compare information found on different Web sites side-by-side, rather than linearly, using the Back and Forward buttons.
- Provides access to bookmarks from any computer. Online bookmarking facilitates instruction for the teacher who "floats," or who travels to the computer lab for a lesson. Online bookmarking is an easy way for teachers to access useful sites away from school when creating lesson plans.
- Provides a place for teachers to save and organize sites that they may find at workshops or attending a university for later use.
- Provides an easy way for teachers to share favorite sites with colleagues.

Exhibit Center

In this section, we will highlight the various ways of bookmarking both in the two most popular Web browsers, Internet Explorer and Netscape, as well as examples from several Web-based bookmark management sites including Backflip <http://www.backflip.com>, iKeepBookmarks <http://www.ikeepbookmarks.com>, and MyBookmarks <http://www.mybookmarks.com>. Additionally, we will show examples of two Web browsers, CrystalPort <http://www.crystalport.com> and Opera <http://www.opera.com>, that incorporate tabs that allow multiple Web sites to be opened and viewed at once.

Bookmarking with Internet Explorer

Internet Explorer is one of the most used Web browsers, and it provides a very simple, straightforward way to save and organize bookmarks. With the use of folders, it is a breeze to organize Web sites you have collected into a manageable list.

Figure 2.1: Favorites Menu

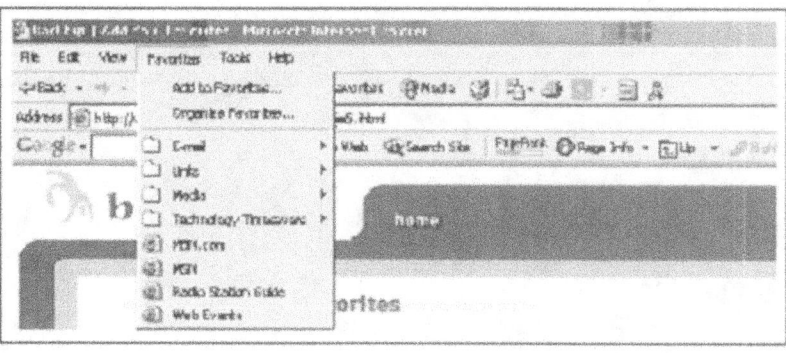

Screen shot reprinted by permission from Microsoft Corporation.

By clicking on the Favorites menu, the sites you have bookmarked are easily accessible. By clicking on the Favorites button on the toolbar, you can also access bookmarked sites. The Favorites button opens a small window to the left of the screen that contains a list of bookmarked sites.

Figure 2.2: Favorites Button

When using the Favorites menu, simply placing the mouse pointer over a folder will display the contents of that folder.

Screen shot reprinted by permission from Microsoft Corporation.

Figure 2.3: Looking in a Folder

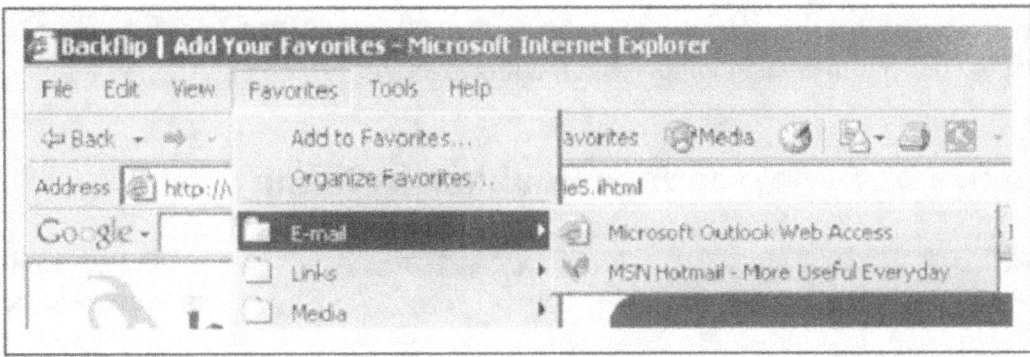

Screen shot reprinted by permission from Microsoft Corporation.

Using the Favorites button simply requires that you click one time on a folder to expand it and view the contents.

Figure 2.4: Expanding a Folder

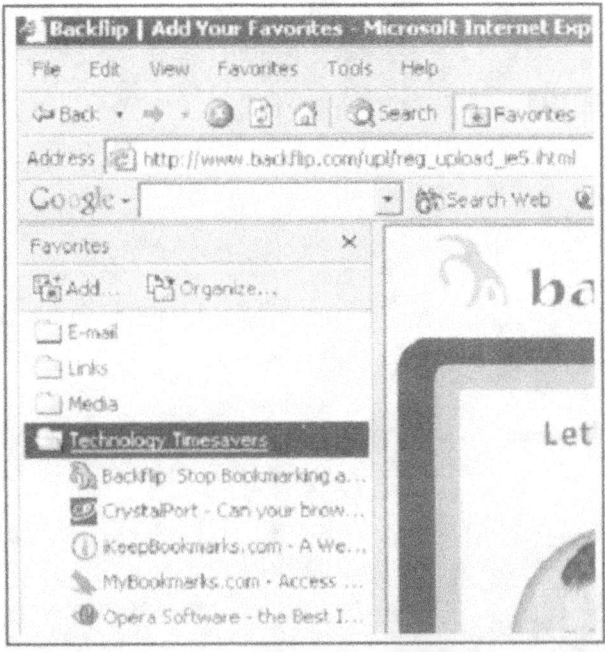

Screen shot reprinted by permission from Microsoft Corporation.

Chapter 2: Organize It: Managing Bookmarks **15**

Bookmarking with Netscape

The Netscape Web browser also provides one-click access to Web sites that you have bookmarked under a menu and button with the same name!

Figure 2.5: The Netscape Bookmarks Menu

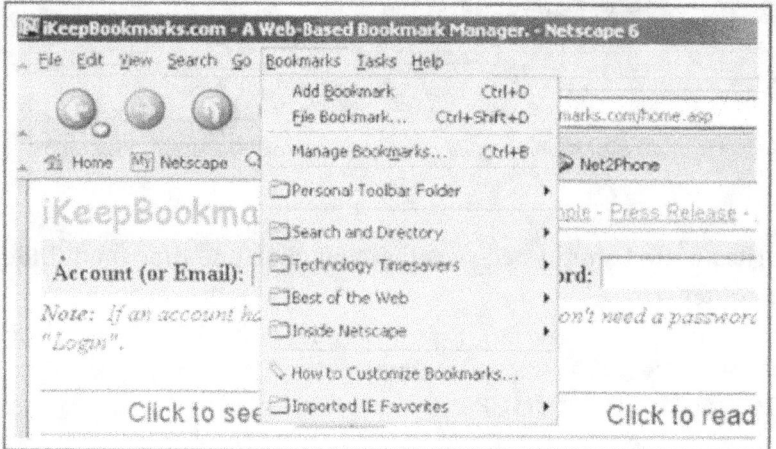

Netscape also provides a feature called the sidebar in its latest browsers that enables you to access bookmarked Web sites in much the same way as Internet Explorer.

Figure 2.6: Netscape Sidebar

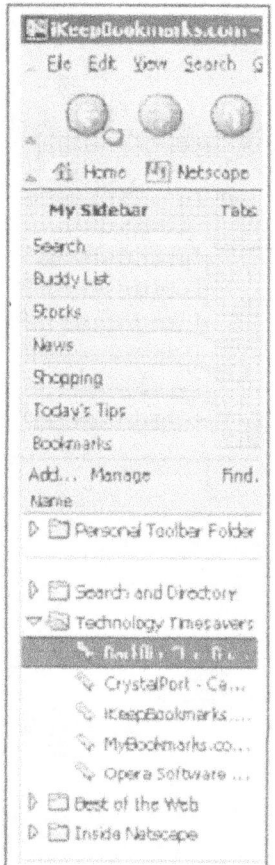

Web-Based Bookmark Management

As mentioned earlier, saving and organizing bookmarks need not be restricted to an individual computer. With the ability to use free services that allow you to create and store your bookmarks on the Web, accessing, sharing, and organizing your favorite sites adds a new dimension to bookmarking. Below are examples of three Web sites that offer Web-based bookmark management for free. (Don't forget! We will show you how to use these in just a minute!)

Figure 2.7: Backflipping Bookmarks

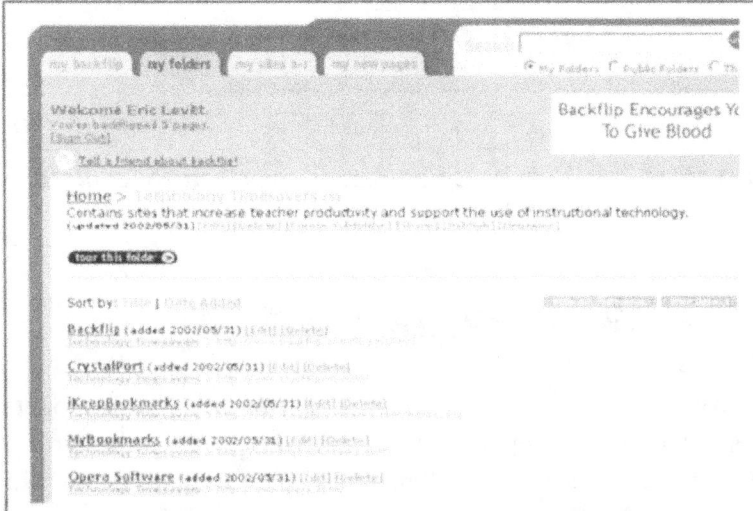

After creating a folder and adding some bookmarks, these sites can be accessed from any computer connected to the Internet.

Figure 2.8: Bookmarking with iKeepBookmarks

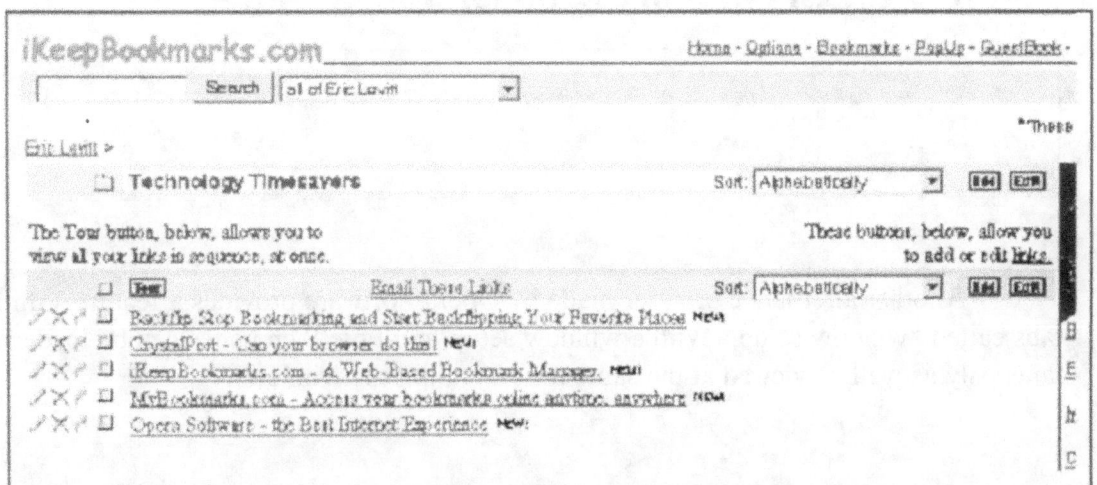

In this example, iKeepBookmarks offers a free service to manage bookmarks on the Web and targets educators by allowing schools to register and to make their folders and bookmarks available to everyone at the school.

Figure 2.9: Bookmarking with MyBookmarks

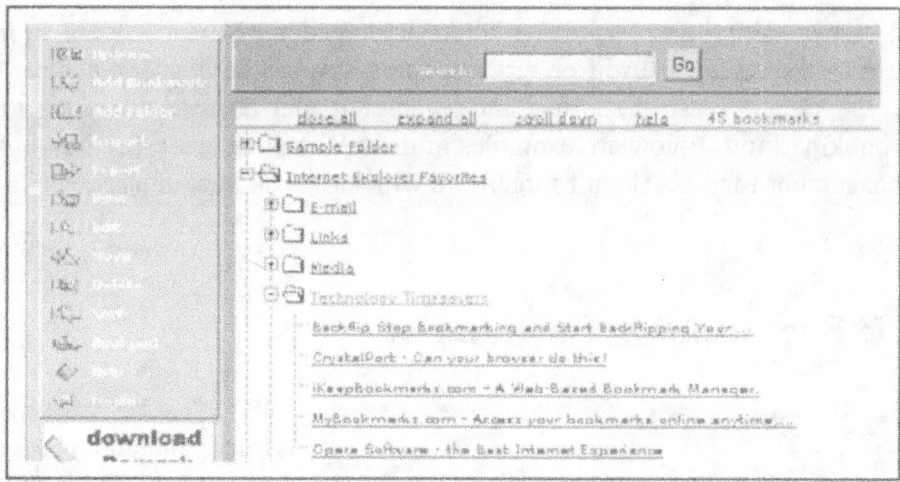

MyBookmarks also offers free Web-based bookmark management and offers a different but user-friendly interface.

Tabs: A New Look at Bookmarking

Using Web browsers like CrystalPort or Opera, you can save similar Web sites together in groups called "tabs." When a tab group is opened, all of the Web pages in that group load into one browser window and can be viewed simultaneously. The example below illustrates how a tab group containing all of the sites from an online activity on Edgar Allan Poe can be opened at the same time in one window.

Figure 2.10: CrystalPort Browser Tab Group

Another alternative browser made by Opera Software provides a feature similar to tabs called "window setup." With a window setup, multiple Web pages can be loaded simultaneously as well as viewed at the same time by tiling the windows.

Figure 2.11: Tiled Windows in Opera Software Web Browser

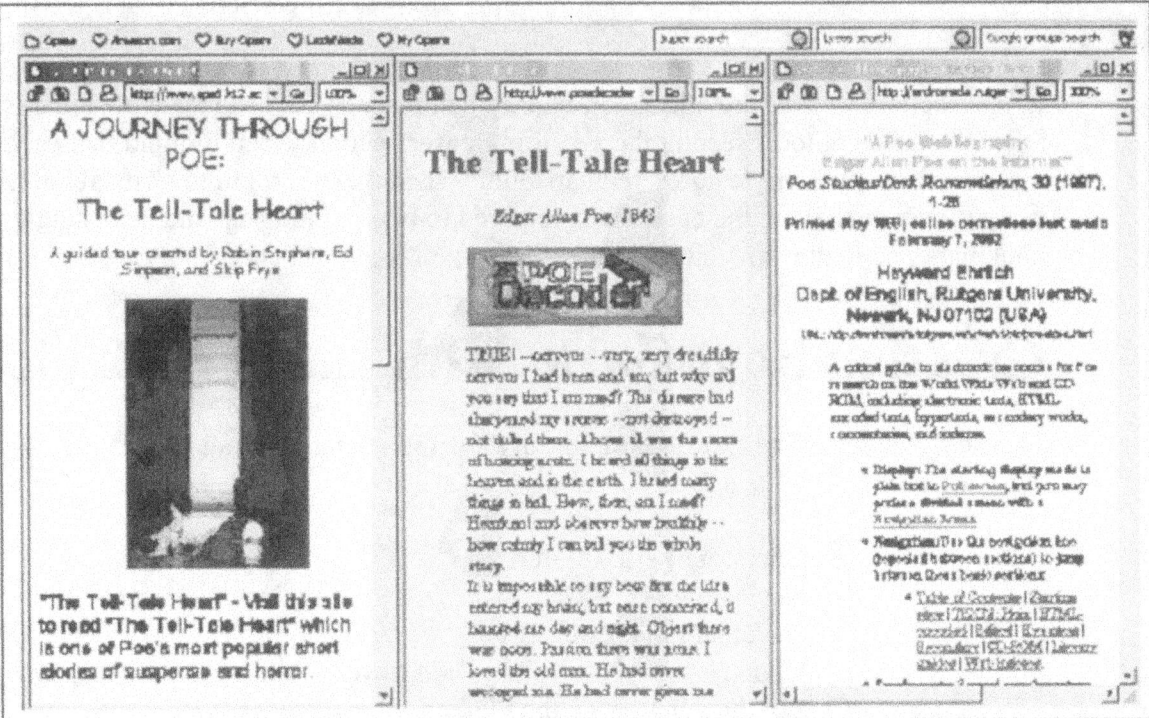

Saving Favorites to a Floppy Disk

For the busy educator, sometimes the easiest way to make sure you have access to your favorites at any time is to copy them to a floppy disk. By copying them to a disk, you can access your favorites by pulling-up the contents of the disk on any computer that has an Internet connection. The steps for saving your favorites to a floppy disk are given below.

1. Launch Internet Explorer.
2. Click on the File menu.
3. Select Import and Export.
4. Click Next at the welcome screen.
5. Select Export Favorites on the next screen.
6. Select the folder from which to export (to get all of your favorites just select the top folder named Favorites).
7. Click Next.
8. Click the Browse button and select the A:/Drive (floppy disk) from the dropdown menu.
9. Make sure there is a disk in drive A: and then click save.
10. Now, simply bring that disk with you anywhere and pull up your favorites by navigating to the A:/ drive and opening up your bookmarks file!

Show Me How It's Done

In this section, we will provide a step-by-step summary of how to create bookmarks using all of the different tools seen in the **Exhibit Center** section. Keep in mind that each of these tools offers many more features and capabilities than there is room to write about here. Our interest is in describing the basic steps required to begin setting-up and accessing your bookmarks no matter which tool or combination of tools you choose to use.

Creating Bookmarks with Internet Explorer

Internet Explorer offers an easy, straightforward approach to storing bookmarks. A couple of ways to accomplish this task are as follows.

1. Open Internet Explorer.
2. Navigate to a Web site, using a search engine if necessary, to locate a useful and interesting site.
3. Upon finding a Web site to add to your Favorites, click one time on the Favorites button on the toolbar.

Figure 2.12: Favorites Button

Screen shot reprinted by permission from Microsoft Corporation.

4. Any existing bookmarked sites will open in a window to the left of the screen and will display any folders or files that have already been created.

Figure 2.13: Favorites Window

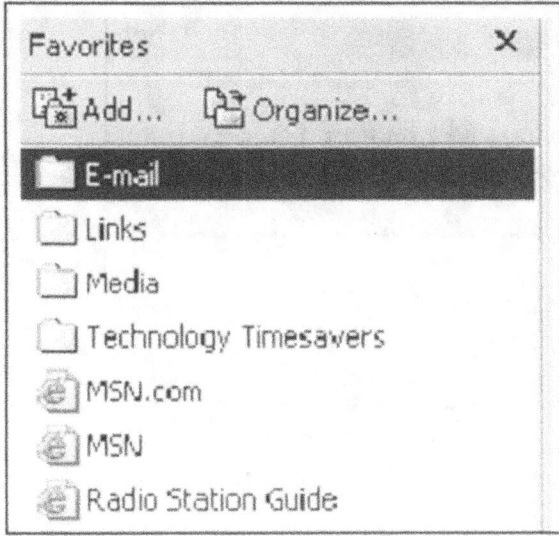

5. Click on the Add button one time.
6. A pop-up window will appear that displays the name of the site that is being bookmarked. It will also provide the opportunity to place the bookmark in an existing folder or to create a new folder in which to place the new bookmark.

Screen shot reprinted by permission from Microsoft Corporation.

Figure 2.14: Adding a Favorite

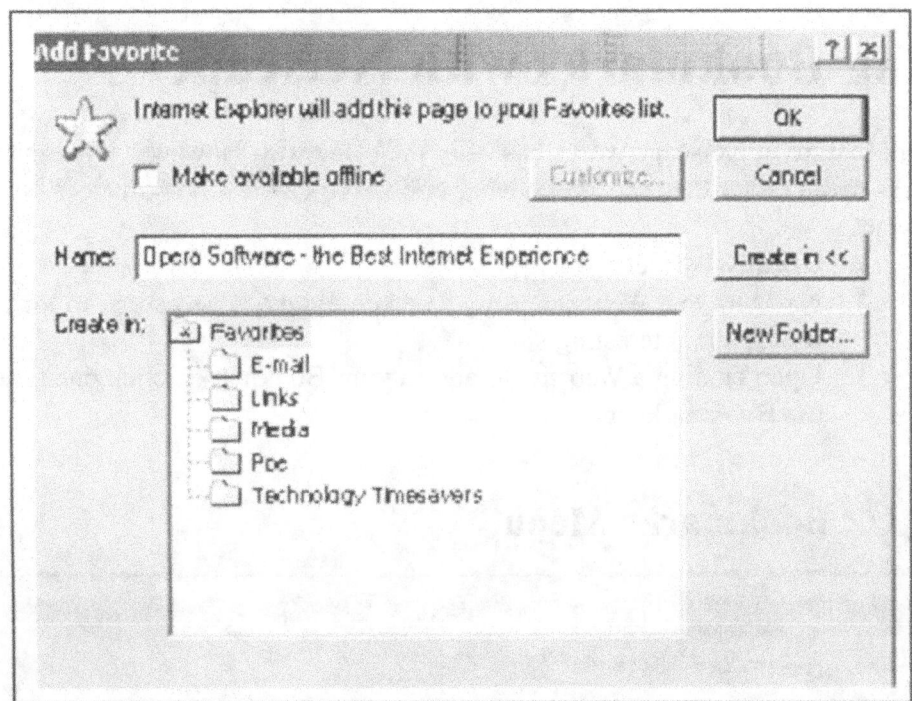

Screen shot reprinted by permission from Microsoft Corporation.

7. To bookmark the Web site in an existing folder, click one time on a folder and click the OK button one time.
8. To bookmark the Web site in a newly created folder, click one time on the New Folder button and type a folder name.

Figure 2.15: Adding a Folder to Favorites

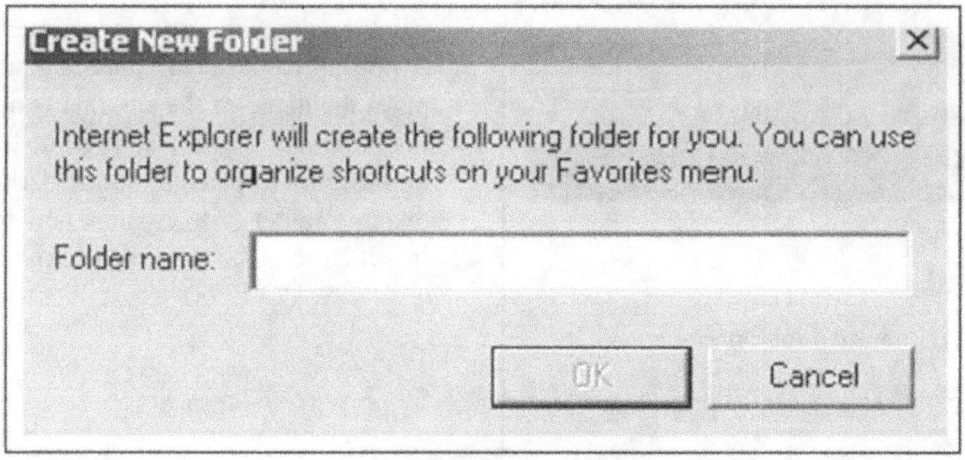

Screen shot reprinted by permission from Microsoft Corporation.

9. The newly created folder will be active and will appear to be open. Click one time on the OK button to create a bookmark.
10. To access your bookmarks, either click on the Favorites menu or click on the Favorites button to navigate to a saved bookmark.

Creating Bookmarks with Netscape

The bookmark feature in Netscape works basically the same way. However, it is easier to use the Bookmarks menu rather than the My Sidebar option. To create a bookmark in Netscape do the following:

1. Open Netscape.
2. Navigate to a Web site, using a search engine if necessary, to locate a useful and interesting site.
3. Upon finding a Web site to add to your Bookmarks, click one time on the Bookmarks menu.

Figure 2.16: Bookmarks Menu

22 Technology Timesavers: Simple Steps to Increasing Classroom Productivity

4. To make sure the bookmark goes into the desired folder, select File Bookmark.
5. A pop-up window will appear that displays the name of the site that is being bookmarked. It will also provide the opportunity to place the bookmark in an existing folder or to create a new folder in which to place the new bookmark.

Figure 2.17: Add Bookmark Window

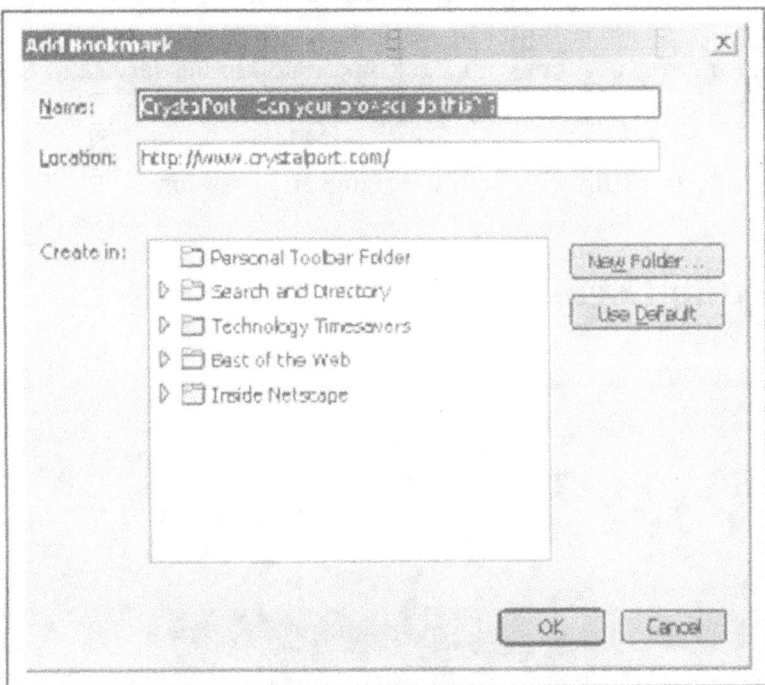

6. To bookmark the Web site in an existing folder, click one time on a folder and click the OK button one time.
7. To bookmark the Web site in a newly created folder, click one time on the New Folder button and type a folder name.

Figure 2.18: Adding a Folder to Bookmarks

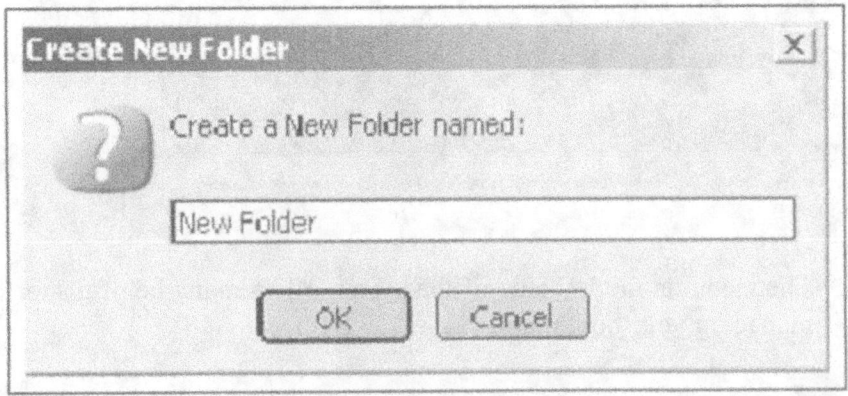

8. The newly created folder will be active and will appear to be highlighted. Click one time on the OK button to create a bookmark.
9. To access your bookmarks, click on the Bookmarks menu and navigate to a saved bookmark.

Using Backflip to Manage Bookmarks Online

Backflip is one of three tools we will show you that enables you to save and organize your bookmarks online. There are several advantages to doing this:

- Bookmarked sites are easily accessible from any Internet-connected computer. There is no worry that bookmarked sites will be accidentally deleted during routine computer maintenance.
- Bookmarked sites are secured by requiring a log on name and password.
- Selected bookmarks can easily be shared with others.

After registering for a free account with Backflip, log on to the service to begin saving and organizing bookmarks.

1. Log on to Backflip with your username and password.

Figure 2.19: Backflip Login

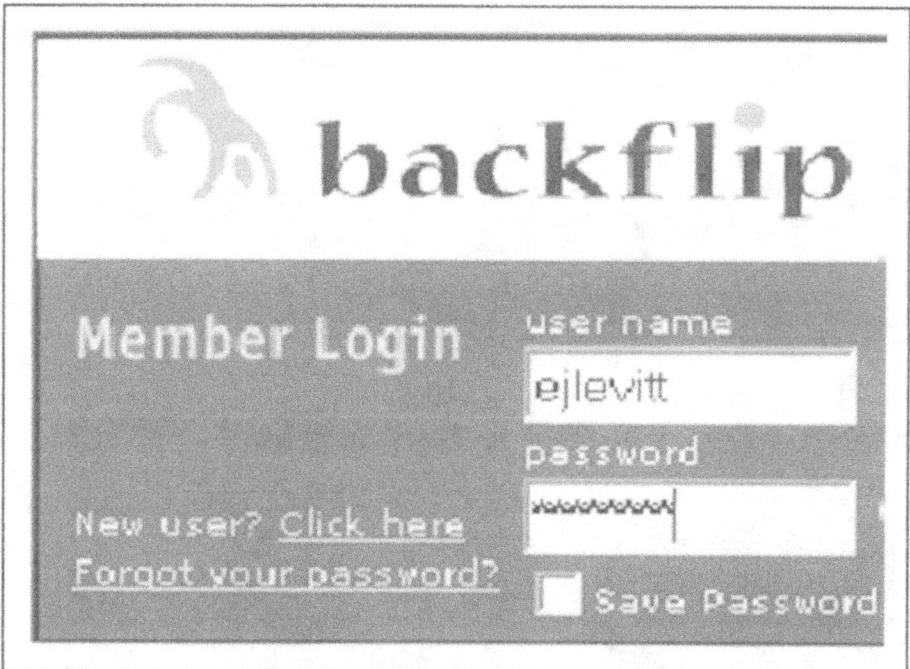

2. The menu on the left side of the screen offers many helpful shortcuts to managing your bookmarks.

Figure 2.20: Backflip Navigation Menu

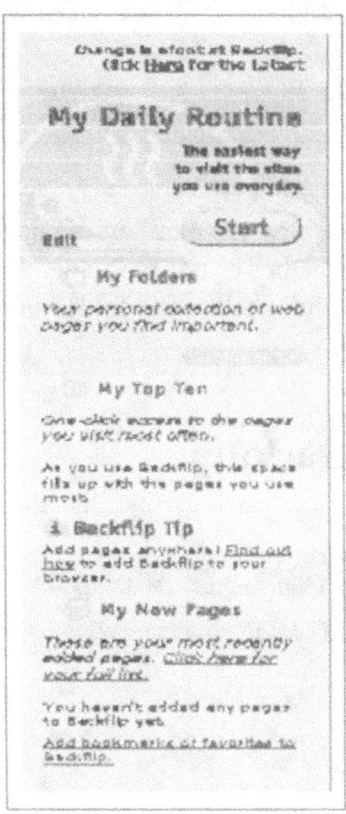

3. Clicking on the My Folders menu item will load a page that contains all of your existing folders (Backflip provides several default folders that can be utilized or deleted). Next to each folder is a number in parentheses that indicates how many sites are stored in that particular folder.

Figure 2.21: My Folders in Backflip

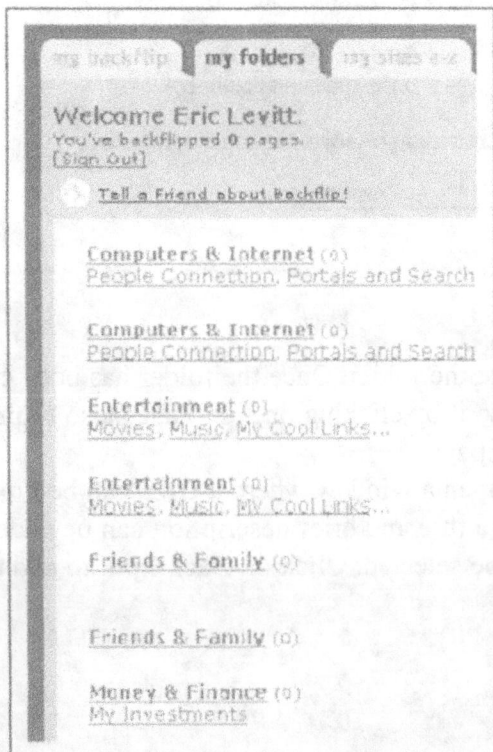

4. To add a new folder to begin organizing your bookmarks, click on Create Folders on the menu at the top of the page.

Figure 2.22: Backflip Management Menu

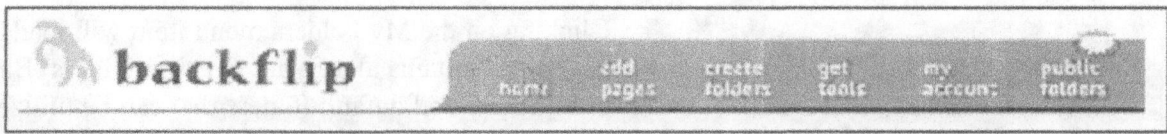

5. A folder setup window will load. It asks you the name of the new folder, an optional description of the folder, whether or not the folder should stand alone or be filed as a subfolder, and whether the folder should be filed as public.

Figure 2.23: Creating a New Folder in Backflip

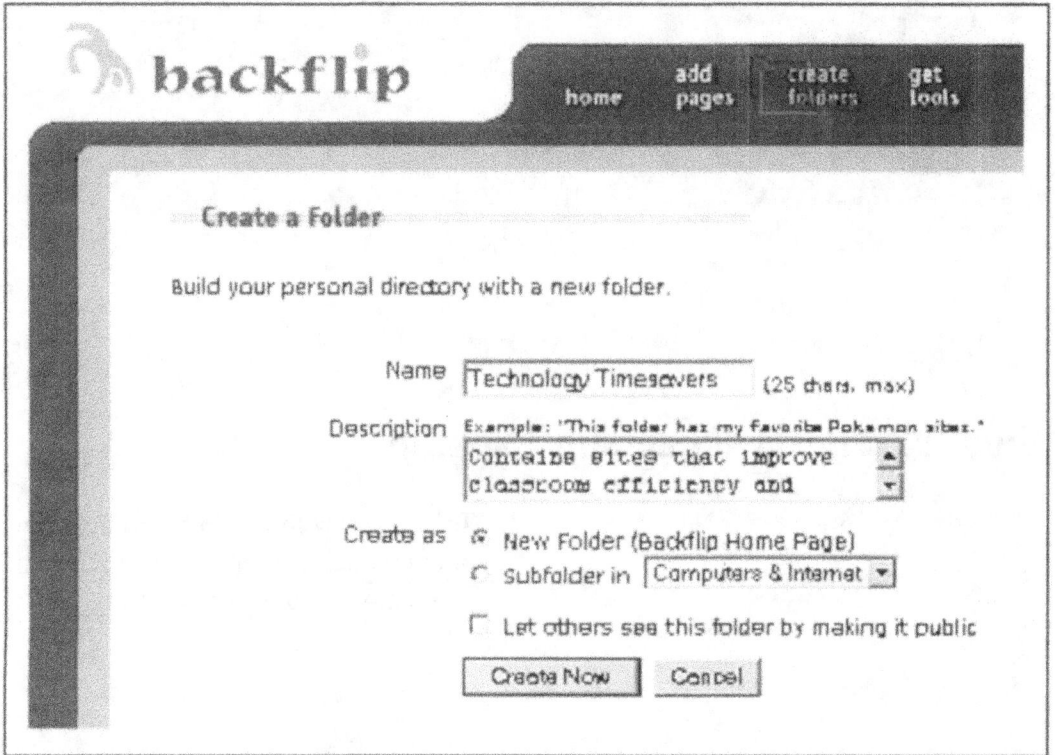

6. Click Create Now to create the folder. Once the folder has been created, begin adding bookmarks to it by clicking on Add Pages also found on the menu at the top of the page.
7. Clicking Add Pages will open a window where a URL can be typed (or copied and pasted in), a title and brief description can be added, and a specific folder can be selected. Click on Backflip it to add the bookmark.

Figure 2.24: Adding a Bookmark to Backflip

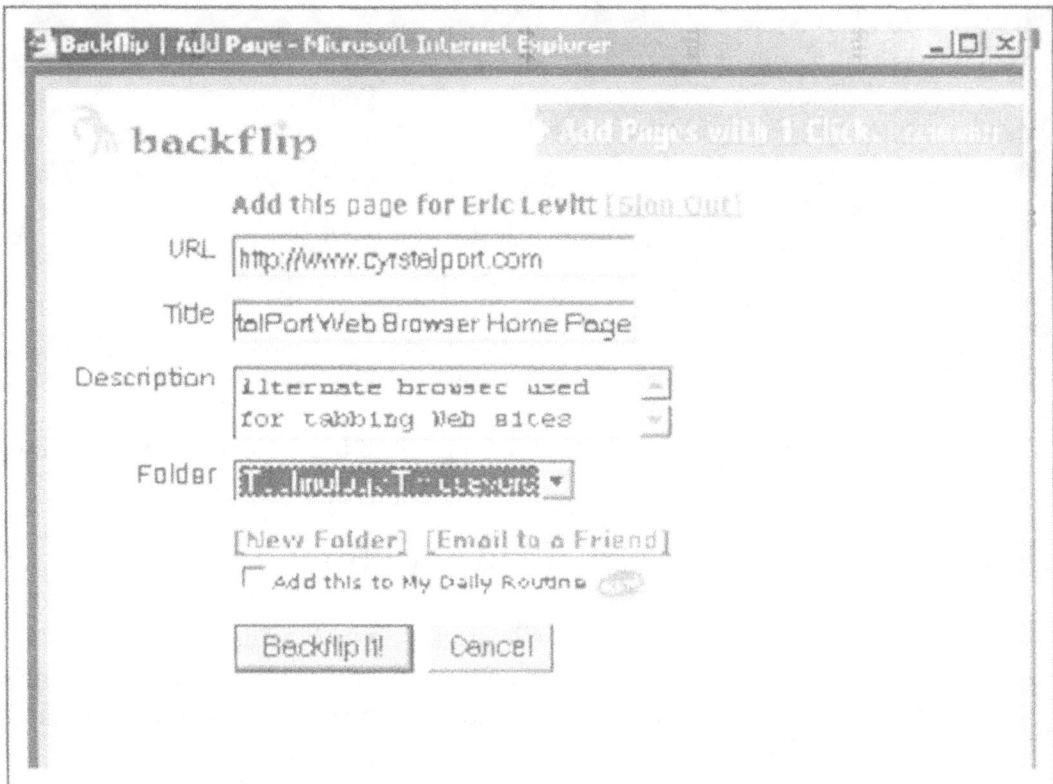

8. To access saved bookmarks in the future, log on to Backflip and navigate to My Folders and locate and click the desired favorite.

Using iKeepBookmarks to Manage Favorites Online

Similar to Backflip, iKeepBookmarks provides a free service that enables saving bookmarks to the Web to be accessed later at any time either privately or publicly when preferred.

After registering for a free account with iKeepBookmarks, log on to the service to begin saving and organizing bookmarks.

1. Log on to iKeepBookmarks at <www.ikeepbookmarks.com> with your account and password.
2. Immediately a window will load displaying all of the current bookmark folders that you have created or imported from your Internet Explorer favorites.

Figure 2.25: Bookmarks in iKeepBookmarks

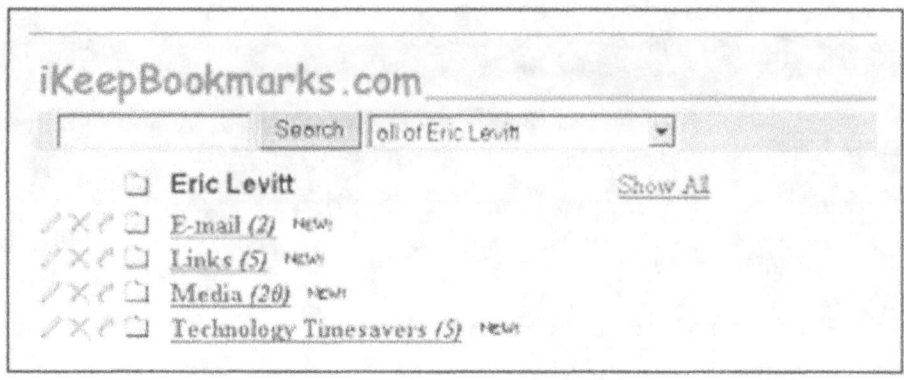

3. To add a new folder, click on the Add button located in the yellow section.

Figure 2.26: Adding a New Folder Button

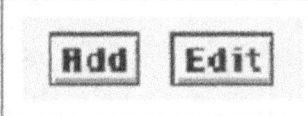

4. A window loads asking you the desired name for the folder, whether or not to lock accessibility to the folder, an optional description, and the option to assign an icon to the folder.

Figure 2.27: Adding a New Folder Screen

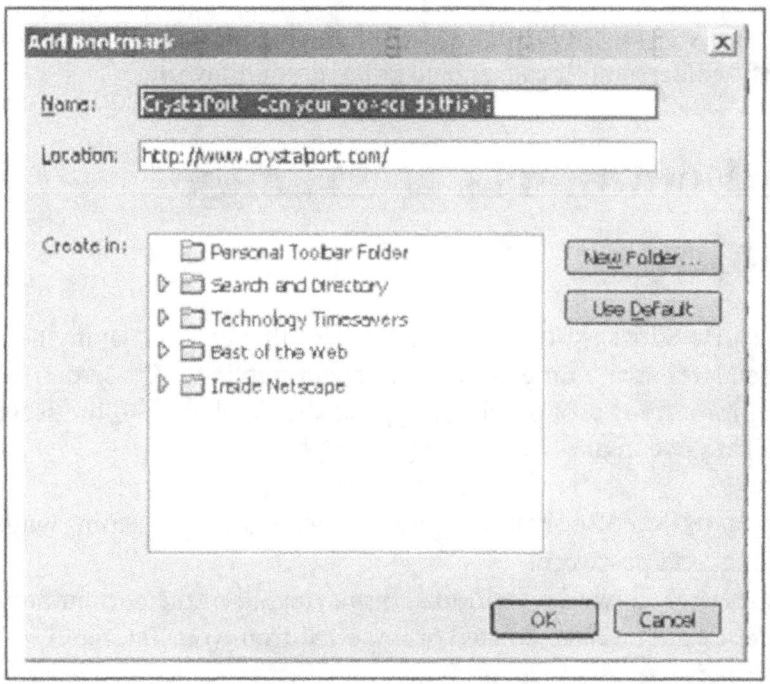

5. Click the Finished button once the information has been provided.
6. To add a bookmark to your newly created folder, click one time on the folder name. This will load a window that displays any bookmarks that are stored in the folder.
7. This time, click the Add button in the green section because you are adding a bookmark and not a folder.

Figure 2.28: Adding a New Bookmark Button

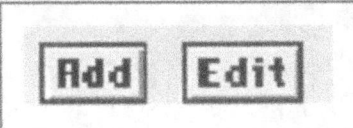

8. A title and URL are required, but the description is optional.

Figure 2.29: Adding a New Bookmark to iKeepBookmarks

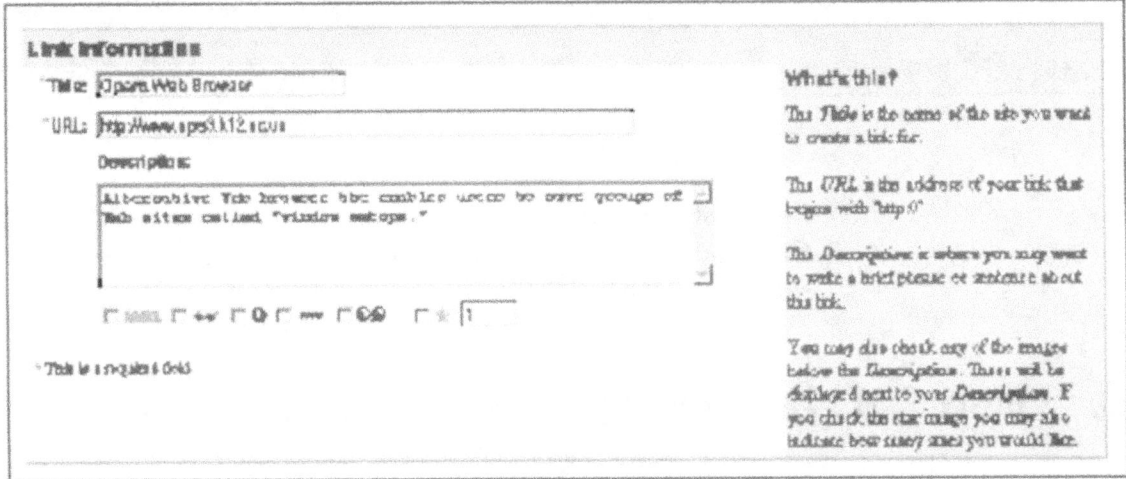

9. Click on Finished and the bookmark will be saved.
10. To access your bookmarks in the future, log on to iKeepBookmarks, and your bookmarks will load right away.

Creating Tab Groups with CrystalPort Web Browser

CrystalPort is a Web browser that is built on Internet Explorer's design. One of the many added features is the ability to create *tab groups*, collections of similar Web sites that can be opened simultaneously and viewed side-by-side in the same window. There are several ways to create tab groups, and the procedure demonstrated here is one of the most straightforward ways.

1. Download the CrystalPort browser from <http://www.crystalport.com>.
2. After saving and installing the CrystalPort software, start the program.
3. Create a folder containing favorites following the same steps as outlined in the section regarding bookmarking using Internet Explorer.
4. Once your folder is complete, it is time to create a tab group.
5. Click on the Tabs menu and select Add a Tab and from the submenu select From Favorites.

Figure 2.30: Adding a Tab from Favorites

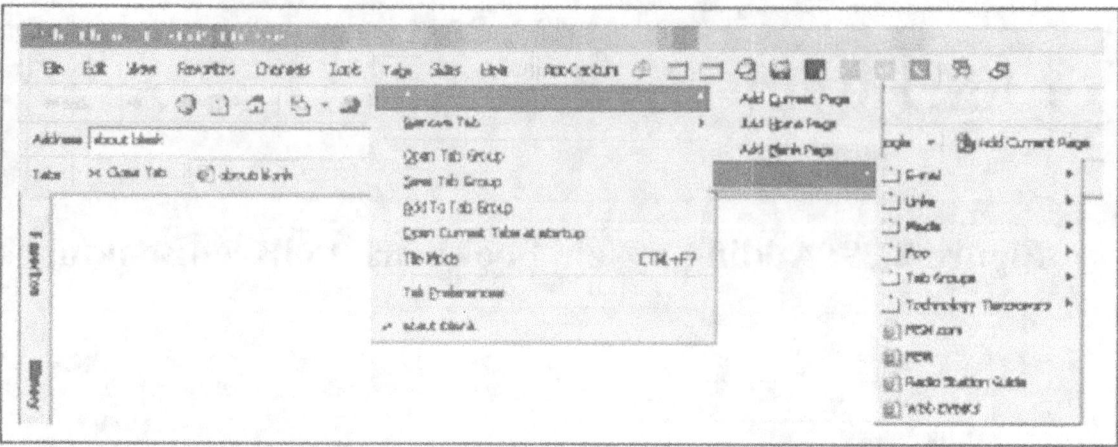

6. Repeat Step 5 as many times as necessary to complete the tab group.
7. Once completed, the tab toolbar will appear with icons for as many Web sites as have been added.

Figure 2.31: Tab Toolbar

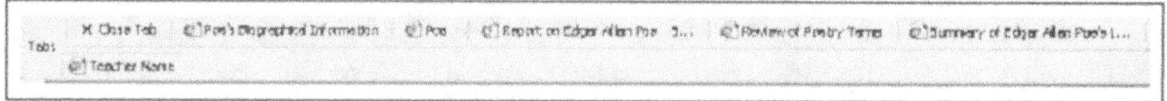

8. To save the tab group, click on the Tabs menu and select Save Tab Group. Provide a name for the tab group and click Save.
9. To view all of the sites in the tab group in one window at the same time, go to the Tabs menu and select Tile Mode.

Figure 2.32: Viewing Tabs in Tile Mode

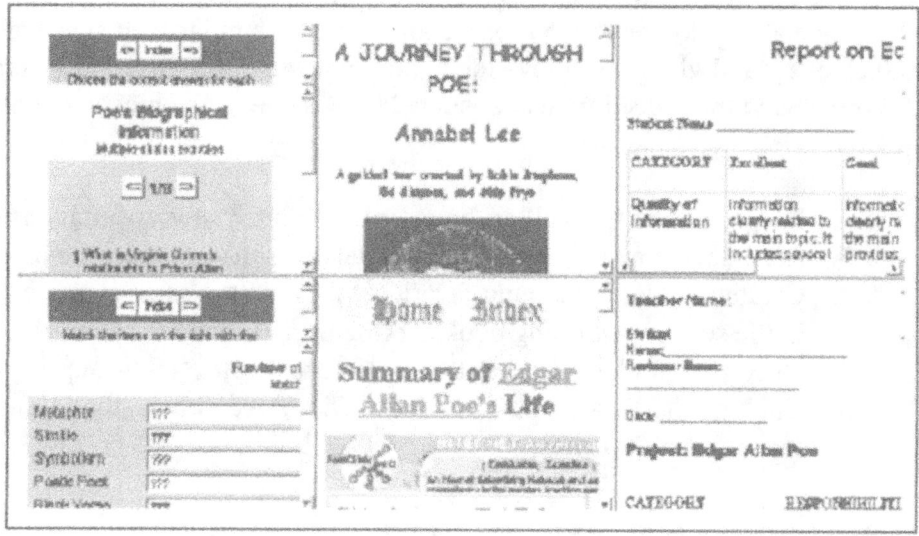

10. To close all of the tabs in the tab group, press the F10 key on the keyboard.
11. To open an existing tab group, go to the Tabs menu and select Open Tab Group. Select the desired tab group from the list.

Creating Saved Window Setups with Opera Web Browser

The Opera Web browser provides a feature similar to tabbing, but this feature is referred to as "saved window setups." Essentially, multiple sites can be loaded into one browser window and can be saved together as a window setup. The process is not as streamlined as CrystalPort, but because the Opera browser remains free past the 30-day trial period that CrystalPort implements, it is a good alternative.

1. Download the Opera browser from <http://www.opera.com/>.
2. After saving and installing the Opera software, start the program.
3. To begin creating a saved window setup, create a group of favorites following the instructions for Internet Explorer.
4. Begin by navigating to the newly created folder and select the first bookmark.
5. The site will load and an icon will appear in the window bar.
6. Locate the icon on the window bar and right-click on it one time.
7. Select Page and then Create Linked Window, which will create a new blank page tab.

Figure 2.33: Window Bar and Creating Linked Windows

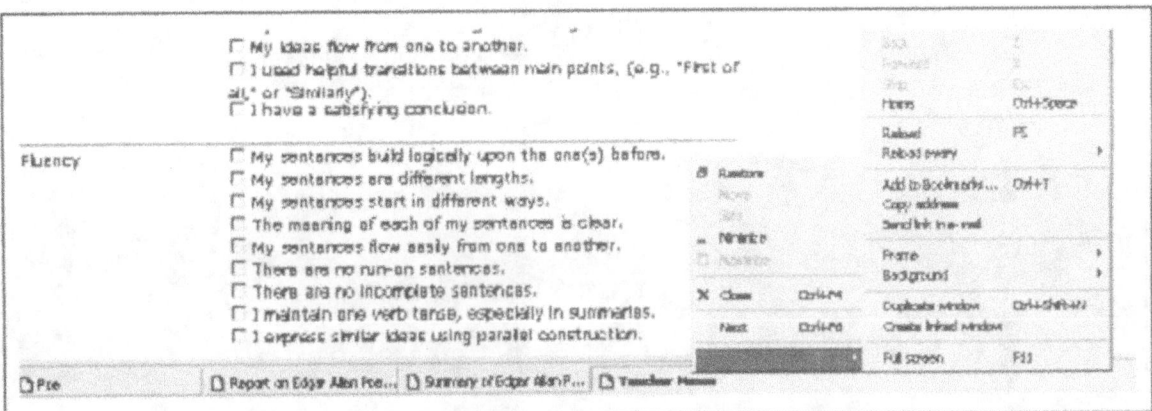

8. Repeat steps 4–7 until all of the sites are loaded on the window bar.
9. To view all of the Web sites loaded, click on the Window menu and choose either Cascade Vertically or Cascade Horizontally.

Figure 2.34: Windows Tiled in Opera Web Browser

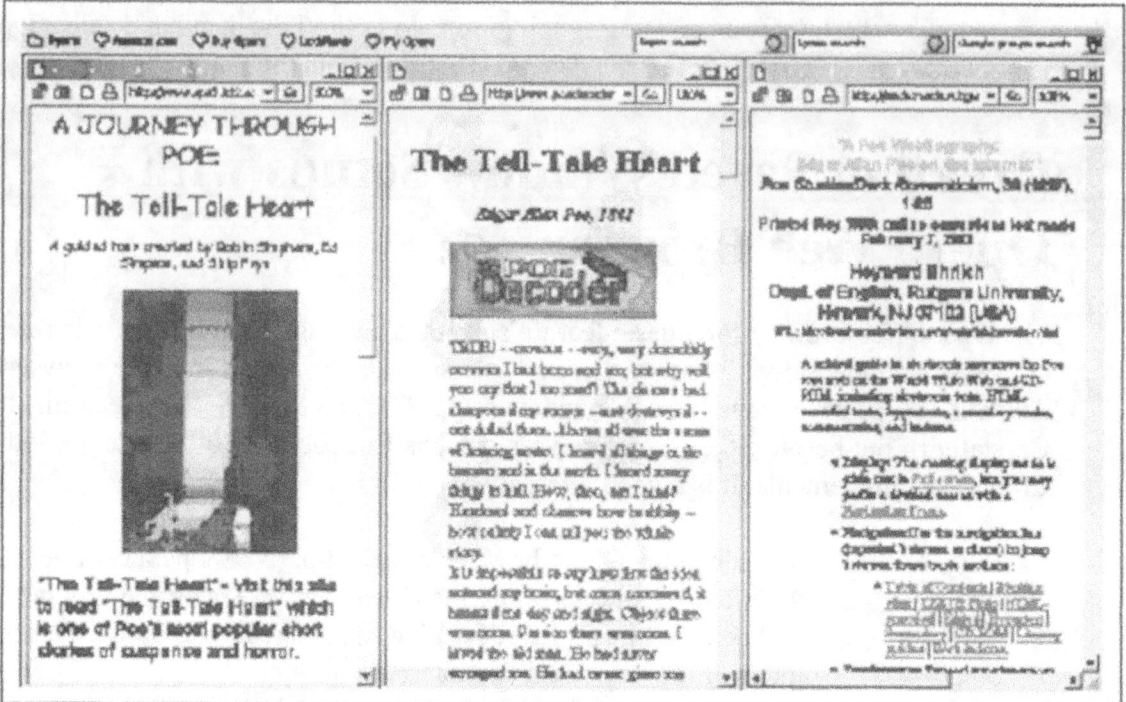

10. To save the window setup, click on the Window menu and select Save window setup.
11. Change the name and location of the file if desired and click OK.
12. To load a saved window setup, click on the File menu and select Open. Navigate to the location of the saved window setup file. Select Opera Window Setup in the Files of Type dropdown box.
13. Double-click the desired window setup file.

Chapter 3

Thinking with Bubbles

> *"The trouble with our times is that the future is not what it used to be."*
>
> —*Paul Valery*

Why Use Inspiration?

The future of how teachers facilitate learning is much different than in the past. Advances in technology and software have provided a face-lift to the instructional strategies that teachers previously employed. As any student who had attended school prior to the explosion of the Internet and personal computers in the mid-1990s would say, assignments were relegated to pencil and paper or dusty chalk examples on a blackboard. Inspiration shatters this old mold and provides a fertile canvas on which students and teachers are able to express complex ideas and explain relationships between concepts by creating highly engaging, visual representations of the thinking process.

During a typical training session on Inspiration, one of the questions that we ask teachers is, *"Why did you sign-up for this particular class?"* A few teachers respond that they need the credit for re-certification or that they want to enhance their technology skills. Inevitably, at least one teacher will say, *"To become inspired."* This half-joking response generally turns out to be true after the teacher has acquired the skill and knowledge to create wonderfully dynamic, imaginative diagrams and graphic organizers that can be used immediately with students in a wide variety of formats.

Although there are other graphic organizer programs available, the multiple features, interactive possibilities, affordable pricing structure, and simple interface are qualities that we value in Inspiration.

Clarify Thinking

Over the past decade, educators have become more aware that students learn in a variety of ways and respond to instruction on many different levels. Recent brain research has established that the brain seeks out patterns.

The theories associated with brain-based learning abound today. Everyone uses the lingo. We know that we need to place information into long-term storage if we wish to retain it for long periods of time. We also know that there is a limit to how much information we can retain in working memory, where we process it before sending it out of the system or into long-term memory. Educators accept this information and use it to a greater or lesser degree.

We all can tell stories about how effective it is to "chunk" information. Chunking is the grouping of information into meaningful pieces. In other words, we take a set of data and work with it as one. The advantage, of course, is that this allows the learner to learn more effectively. When we are forced to process random bits of information, we have difficulty remembering it. Chunking, then, is putting things into groups or categories.

We learn best when we can relate information. This suggests that a thematic lesson may be more effective in assisting students in learning to "chunk" information. As experienced teachers, we do this naturally in the classroom. We normally start with the big themes and break them down into manageable, smaller pieces. The Thinking Maps process allows us to do this with greater efficiency.

As the words and the thoughts interact, shape, and transform each other, we often experience a flash of insight. For many of us, that *"aha"* moment is when we are able to see the relationships between things. At that point, transformation can take place. What we know now can transform what we knew before. Using the thematic approach, the teacher unifies the lesson as it spirals into greater complexity.

By enabling students to quickly generate and record their thoughts using brainstorming and to then refine those thoughts using thinking maps, Inspiration appeals to visual learners who process ideas best through seeing examples. Students need to make the connection between the curriculum and their own world. Visual tools allow them to do this.

Through David Hyerle's work, we have seen the development of Thinking Maps, a process for mapping thinking through eight basic maps. Through the maps, students begin to understand what they are thinking and, most importantly, how they are thinking. As teachers, we try to focus on providing content that will be remembered beyond next week's test or the mid-term.

The eight basic maps in the Thinking Maps process are: circle (defining), bubble maps (describing), double bubble (comparing and contrasting), tree (classifying), brace (breaking the whole into parts), flow (sequencing), multi-flow (determining cause and effect), and bridge (seeing analogies). Inspiration provides easy-to-use templates for all eight maps. Through a fill-in-the-blank approach, teachers can modify these templates for use in their classes. Teachers who have not been exposed to Thinking Maps training should feel comfortable in using the templates.

Figure 3.1: Brace Map

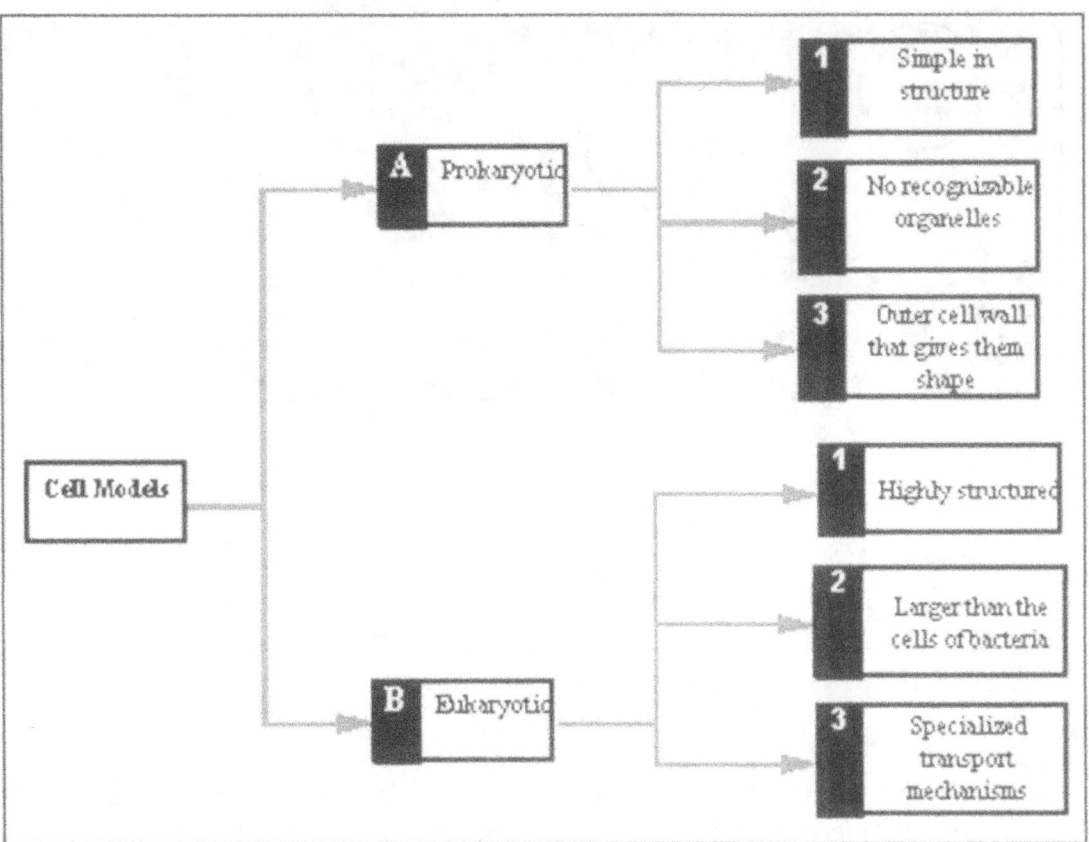

As many educators can testify, students often come to the classroom lacking organizational skills. This lack of organization reaches beyond the typical missing pencil or lost piece of paper. Although most students are bright and enthusiastic, many students (particularly middle school students) have difficulty organizing their thinking. Their thought processes could best be described as chaotic.

Sample Applications

Inspiration offers these students, who often struggle with traditional methods of classroom instruction, a way to literally see their thoughts generated right before their eyes and provides them an opportunity to manipulate and organize their thoughts in a way that has purpose and meaning.

Using a double-bubble template, students map out what they know about two contrasting ideas. They are able to organize their thinking into what the ideas have in common and how the ideas may be different. Using hurricanes and tornadoes as an example, a necessary first step for a student preparing to write a compare/contrast essay is to think about the similarities and the differences between these two storms. The double-bubble map itself helps organize thinking. Note that the bubbles in the middle of the diagram are qualities that hurricanes and tornadoes have in common with each other.

Figure 3.2: Double Bubble Map

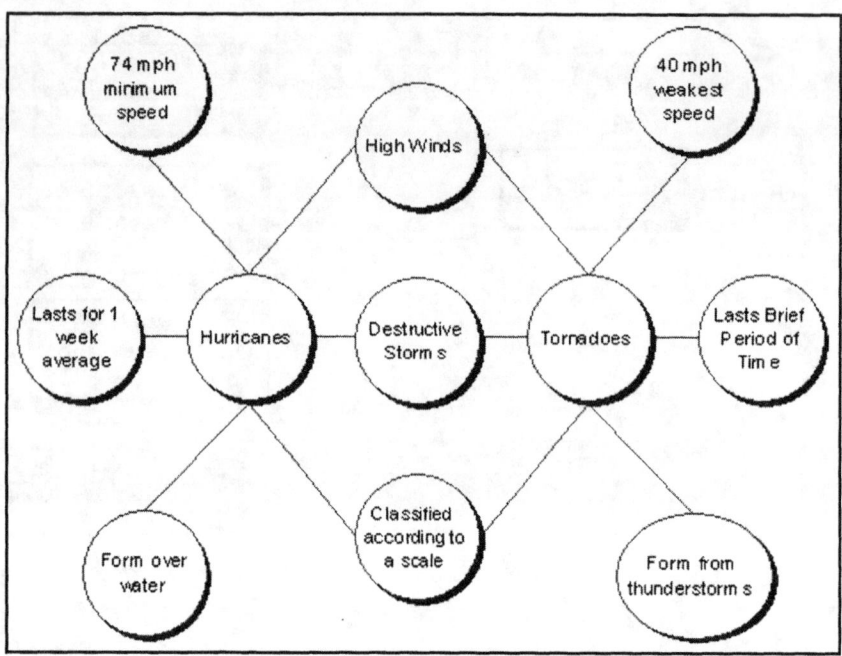

This screen shot, created using Inspiration, published by Inspiration Software, Inc., is reprinted with permission.

For another example, teachers and students can explore a complex topic, such as the causes of the American Civil War. Using a template to help organize thinking, students and teachers map out ideas.

Figure 3.3: Thinking-Idea Map Template

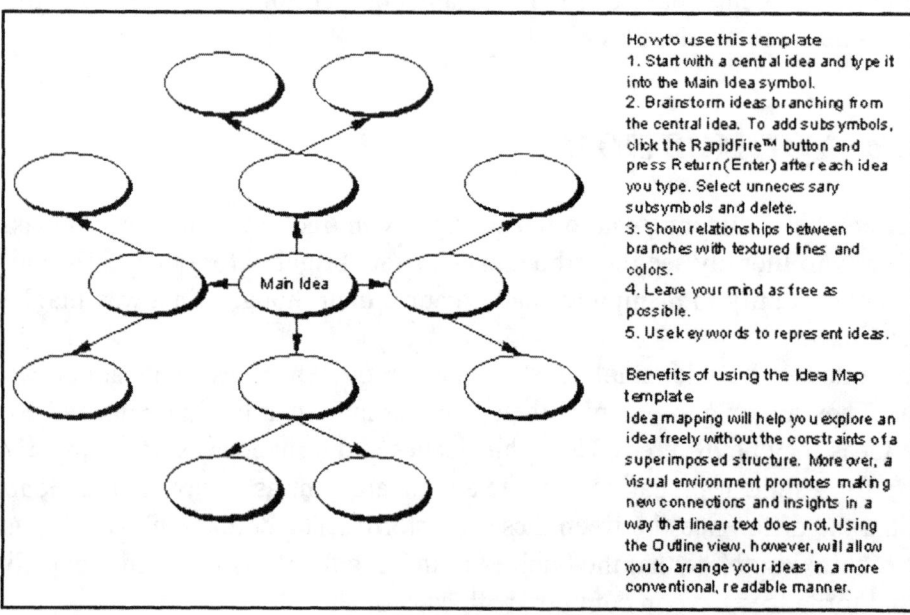

This screen shot, created using Inspiration, published by Inspiration Software, Inc., is reprinted with permission.

Now, students can begin brainstorming ideas just as quickly as they can key the words in the document. The initial result might resemble the completed map in Figure 3.4.

Figure 3.4: Brainstorming the Causes of the American Civil War

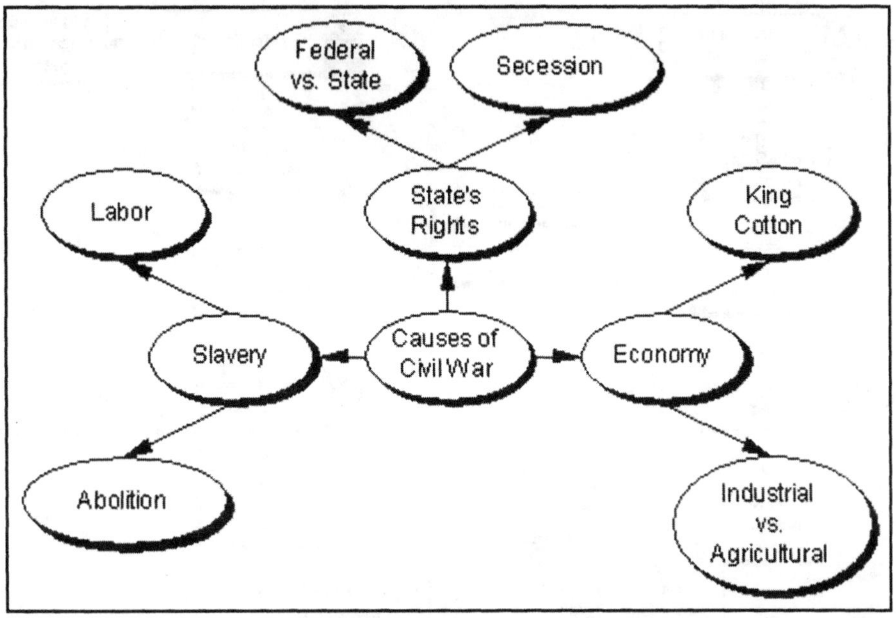

This screen shot, created using Inspiration, published by Inspiration Software, Inc., is reprinted with permission.

Using another ready-made graphic organizer template like the one below, students can quickly begin to formalize their ideas and organize their thinking.

Figure 3.5: Template to Organize Knowledge on the Civil War

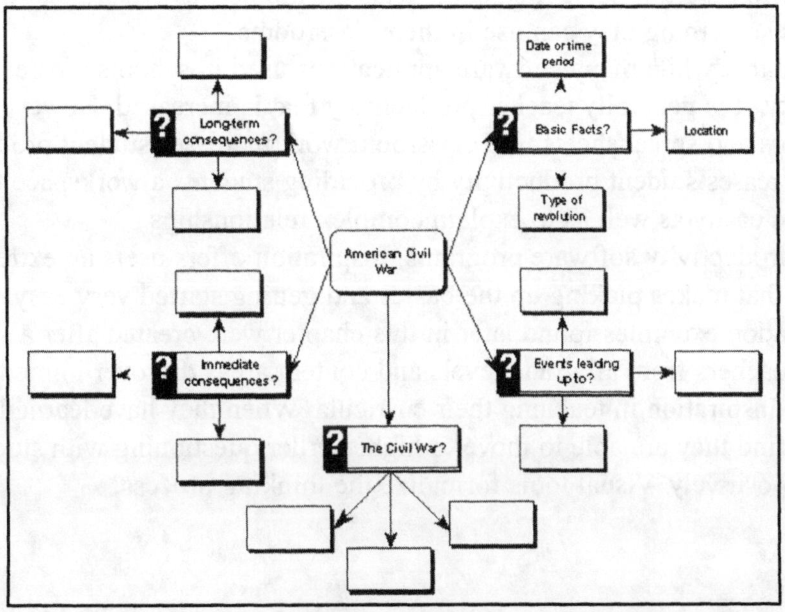

With the broad areas pre-defined, students can work within a structure to organize their thoughts and knowledge.

This screen shot, created using Inspiration, published by Inspiration Software, Inc., is reprinted with permission.

Chapter 3: Thinking with Bubbles 37

Figure 3.6: Causes and Impact of the American Civil War

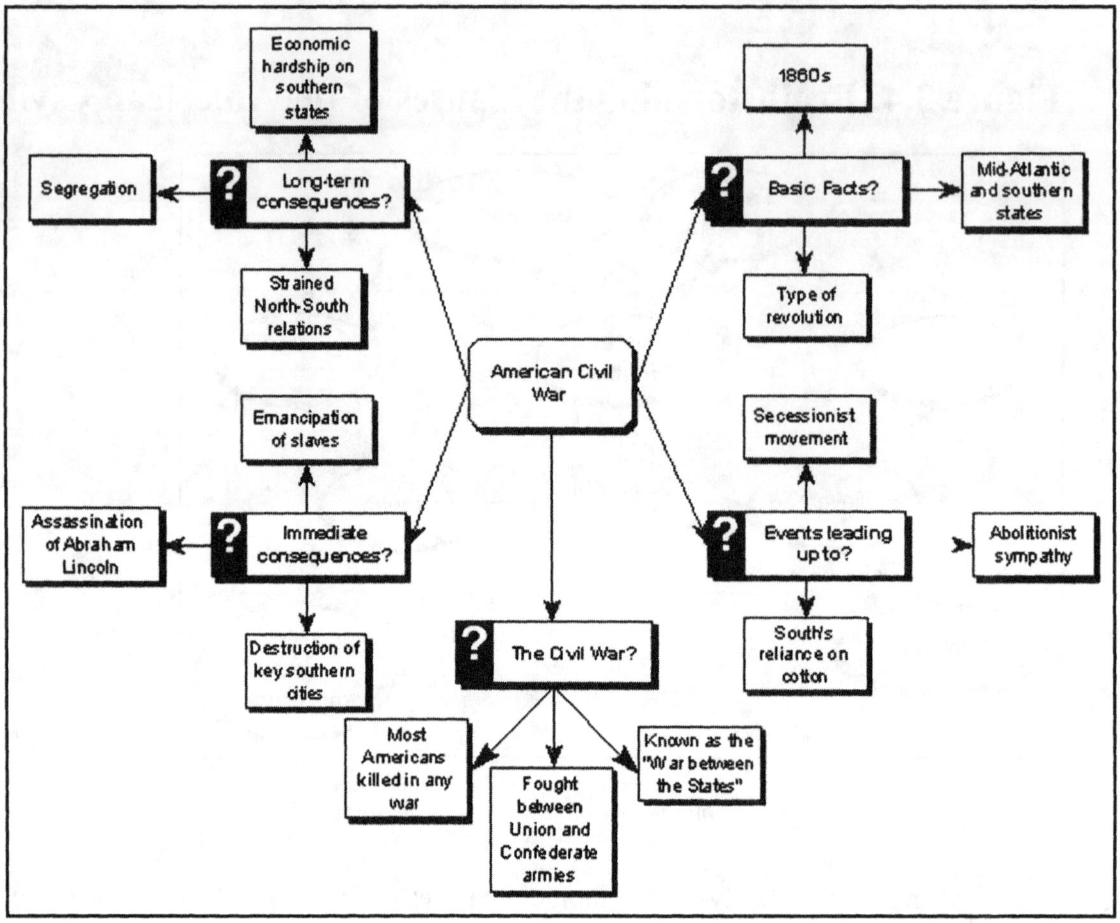

This screen shot, created using Inspiration, published by Inspiration Software, Inc., is reprinted with permission.

Time is valuable. Teachers do not have hours to dedicate to learning how to use software (even if it eventually will save time). At first, some teachers are not really sure that the Inspiration program is something they can use in their classrooms.

We understand that while many software applications used in schools are designed to increase productivity, it is generally teacher productivity that is increased. However, integrating word processors and spreadsheets into classroom work increases student productivity. Inspiration also increases student productivity by providing students a workspace to generate ideas quickly and easily as well as to explain complex relationships.

Unlike some productivity software programs, Inspiration offers users an extremely intuitive environment that makes picking up the basics and getting started very easy. The teacher-created Inspiration examples found later in this chapter were created after a short introductory lesson. Teachers from all grade levels and content areas discover immediate applications for using Inspiration in teaching their curricula. When they have learned to use visual tools, teachers find they are able to move to higher-order questioning with students, and students respond positively. Visual tools formalize the thinking process.

Background Using Inspiration

One of the great features of Inspiration is the speed at which students and teachers acquire the skills necessary to create thinking diagrams. One of the most effective ways to introduce Inspiration to students is to have them work with it in a guided activity. On several occasions when we have assisted teachers during a lesson using Inspiration, the teacher asks students to brainstorm and then we call on students to come to the computer at the front of the room to insert a symbol and text that represent the ideas being generated. Because kids often have no fear of technology, students are able to quickly and adeptly create the diagram with minimal assistance.

What makes Inspiration such a versatile program is the ability to publish the final product, whether it is a thinking map, brainstorm, or character analysis. It is also easy to make adjustments. An Inspiration-created diagram can be "retooled" as thinking becomes more in depth.

Exhibit Center

Examples of Inspiration as a Classroom Tool

The following examples illustrate the practical use of Inspiration and the variety of classroom teachers who have enthusiastically embraced its educational potential.

Figure 3.7: Brainstorming Results of Harvesting of the Rain Forest

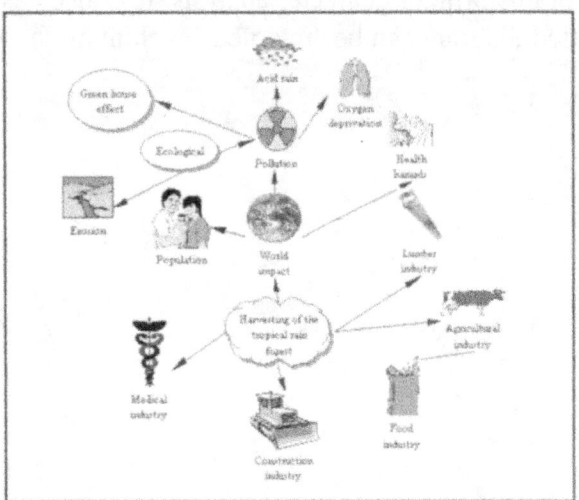

This screen shot, created using Inspiration, published by Inspiration Software, Inc., is reprinted with permission.

Figure 3.8: Exploring Impact of Deforestation

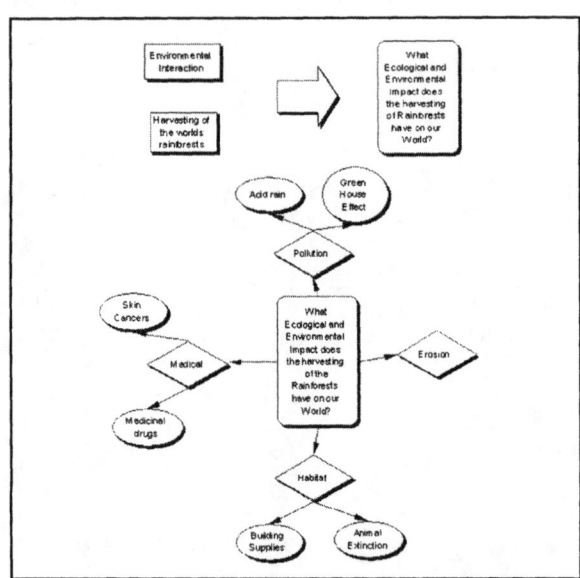

This screen shot, created using Inspiration, published by Inspiration Software, Inc., is reprinted with permission.

Figure 3.9: Brainstorming Basic Needs of Animals Unit

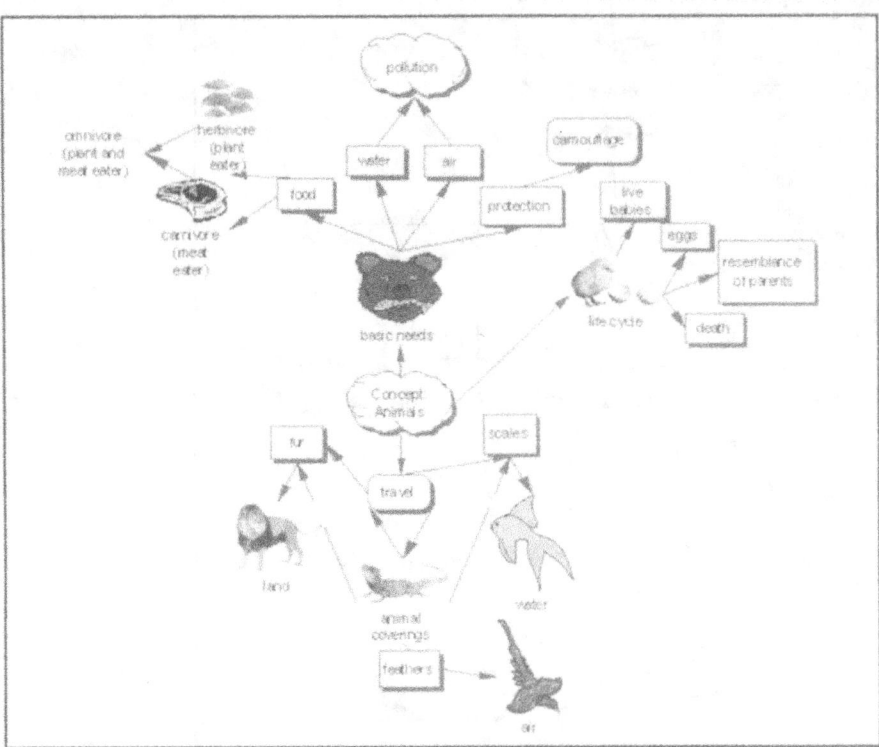

This screen shot, created using Inspiration, published by Inspiration Software, Inc., is reprinted with permission.

Figure 3.10: Animal Survival Guided Tour

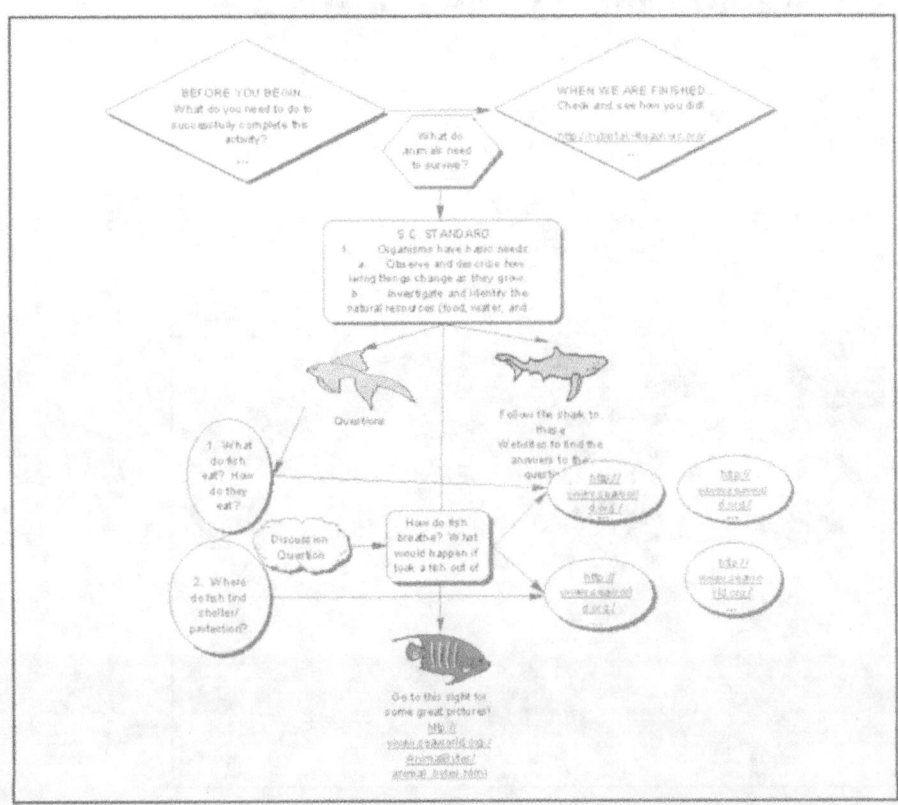

This screen shot, created using Inspiration, published by Inspiration Software, Inc., is reprinted with permission.

Figure 3.11: Brainstorming Animal Survival Needs

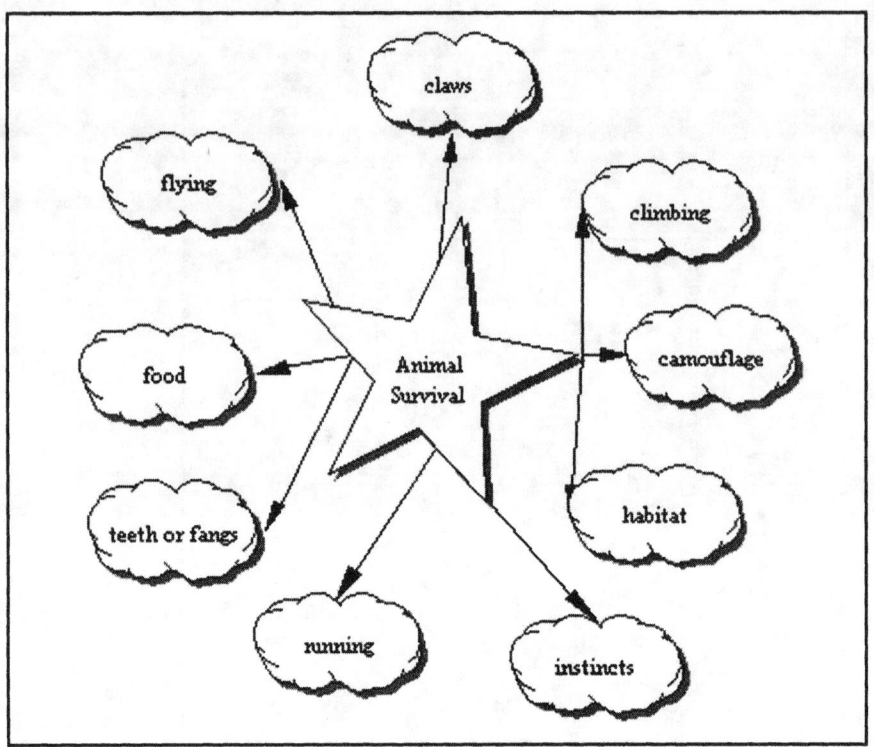

This screen shot, created using Inspiration, published by Inspiration Software, Inc., is reprinted with permission.

Figure 3.12: Brainstorming Causes of Weather

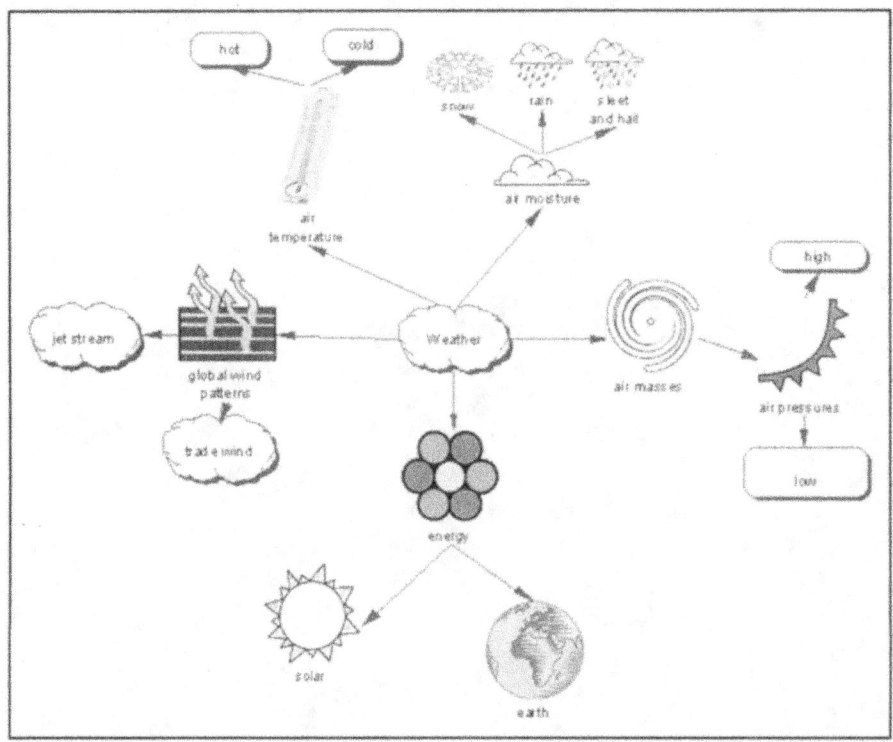

This screen shot, created using Inspiration, published by Inspiration Software, Inc., is reprinted with permission.

Show Me How It's Done

This section will introduce users new to Inspiration to the basic steps required to create a diagram, add and modify symbols, link ideas, and publish an Inspiration diagram. By allowing the user to quickly and easily map ideas, brainstorm concepts, and diagram everything from character analyses of novel characters to historical cause and effect, Inspiration is an ideal tool for classroom discussion, collaborative student activities, and individual outlining. Inspiration is useful to computer users at every level because of the flexibility of the software. By combining word processing with multimedia functionality, Inspiration allows users to develop diagrams as complex or as basic as is needed. Because the software is so versatile, this section will cover the essentials involved in getting started.

What Is Inspiration?

Inspiration is a graphical program that allows the user to insert, onto a canvas, symbols that represent ideas. This is merely the beginning. Symbols in Inspiration come in all shapes and sizes as well as in the form of meaningful images and clipart. If a desired symbol is not available in Inspiration's extensive library of symbols, called the symbol palette, it is quite easy to copy and paste a graphic found on the Internet or to use scanned images or other sources of clipart in an Inspiration document. Once a user begins to fill the canvas with symbols that represent ideas and concepts, organizing and explaining the relationships between the symbols in the diagram is quite simple.

Students or teachers are able to type text descriptions underneath symbols, to label them, and to insert arrows that explain the flow and direction of thoughts and ideas. The graphics automatically expand as text is typed into the square or bubble. Arranging diagrams into meaningful visual interpretations is only one click away.

For students creating an outline for a term paper, Inspiration enables the user to instantly convert a diagram into a traditional, text-only outline format. Or, a student can begin typing an outline in the traditional format, and with one click he or she can change the outline into a graphic diagram containing symbols for ideas and arrows to indicate connections between and among ideas. As a user becomes accustomed to using Inspiration, it is surprisingly easy to modify diagrams to create visually stirring presentations and activities. With the ability to quickly change colors, font styles and sizes, as well as resize and move around symbols, Inspiration diagrams quickly take on a unique, personalized style that allows students to express themselves in new and exciting ways.

Getting Started

Starting a new diagram in Inspiration is similar to opening a word processing document. This tutorial assumes that Inspiration is loaded on the personal computer being used. When Inspiration is launched, the user will see the screen shown in Figure 3.13.

Figure 3.13: Inspiration Screen

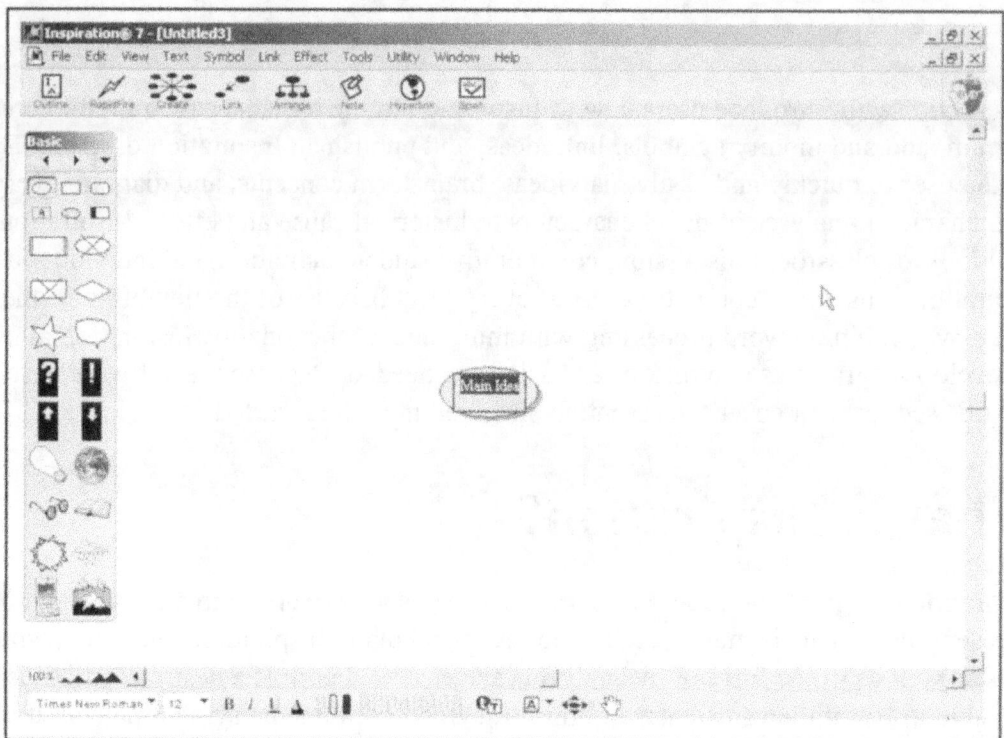

This screen shot, created using Inspiration, published by Inspiration Software, Inc., is reprinted with permission.

The symbol located in the middle of the screen is the main idea symbol and will be the starting point for every new diagram.

Adding Text to a Symbol

When adding text to a newly created symbol, the user simply needs to begin typing. Notice that the text box located inside the symbol is highlighted in black.

Figure 3.14: Main Idea

Whatever is typed will be placed within the symbol. To register the text, click one time on a blank area of the screen. The result may look like Figure 3.15.

This screen shot, created using Inspiration, published by Inspiration Software, Inc., is reprinted with permission.

Figure 3.15: Continents

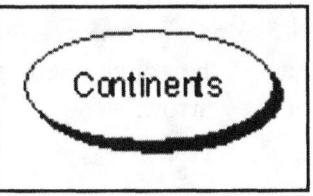

In Inspiration, symbols and graphics can be repositioned by clicking with the mouse on a symbol or graphic and holding the button down while dragging the symbol or graphic.

This screen shot, created using Inspiration, published by Inspiration Software, Inc., is reprinted with permission.

Insert a New Symbol

To begin building a diagram, new symbols will be added to the work area. To insert a new symbol, do the following:
1. Click the mouse one time on the screen in the location where the new symbol should go.
2. Begin typing the new text. As text is entered, a new symbol will automatically appear.
3. Click and drag the new symbol to reposition if necessary.

The diagram from the example above now looks like this:

Figure 3.16: Adding Ideas

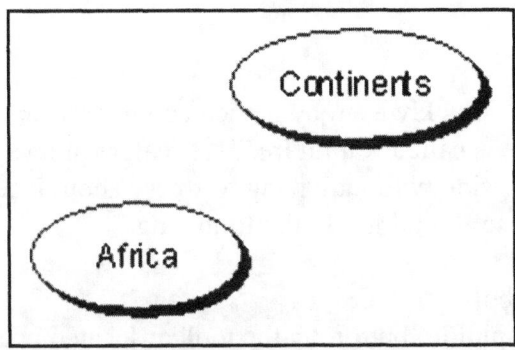

This screen shot, created using Inspiration, published by Inspiration Software, Inc., is reprinted with permission.

Linking Symbols

As symbols are inserted in a diagram, it is useful to show their relationship to one another with the use of connecting arrows. To create a one-way arrow between the main idea and a subordinate idea, do the following:
1. Click one time on the Link button on the toolbar located near the top part of the screen.

Chapter 3: Thinking with Bubbles **45**

Figure 3.17: Link

This screen shot, created using Inspiration, published by Inspiration Software, Inc., is reprinted with permission.

2. The mouse pointer turns into a two-way arrow.
3. Click one time of the main idea and then click one time on the subordinate idea to create a one-way arrow.

Figure 3.18: Creating a Link

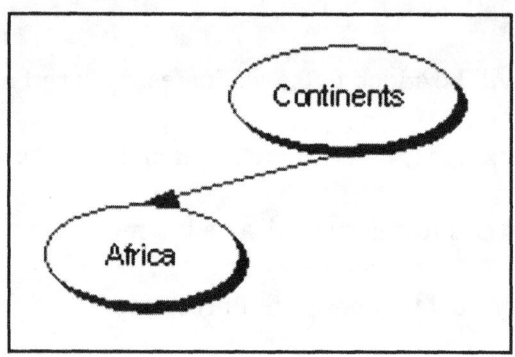

This screen shot, created using Inspiration, published by Inspiration Software, Inc., is reprinted with permission.

4. As new symbols are added, link arrows may used to connect any symbol to any other symbol.

Using RapidFire

As mentioned earlier, Inspiration can be used quickly even by novice computer users. One feature that makes using Inspiration a breeze is called RapidFire. This feature allows users to generate ideas and symbols in rapid succession without having to worry about inserting symbols or creating connecting arrows. To use RapidFire do the following:

1. Click one time on a symbol.
2. Click one time on the RapidFire button on the toolbar located near the top part of the screen.

Figure 3.19: RapidFire

This screen shot, created using Inspiration, published by Inspiration Software, Inc., is reprinted with permission.

3. The symbol will now appear with a red lightning bolt behind the text.

Figure 3.20: Using RapidFire

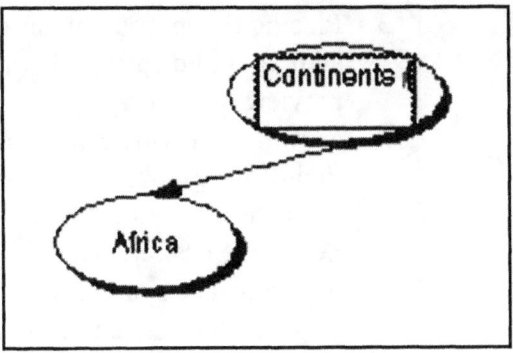

This screen shot, created using Inspiration, published by Inspiration Software, Inc., is reprinted with permission.

4. The cursor will be flashing behind the lightning bolt. Begin typing and press the Enter key on the keyboard after each entry. This will quickly generate a new symbol for each text item entered.

The diagram will now look something like this:

Figure 3.21: RapidFire Diagram

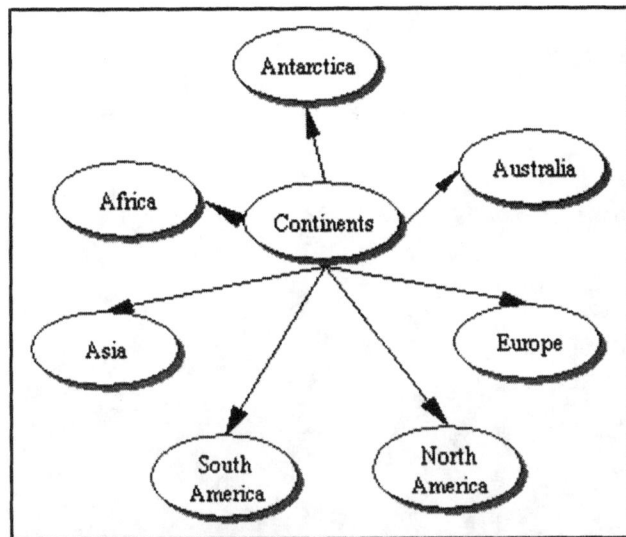

This screen shot, created using Inspiration, published by Inspiration Software, Inc., is reprinted with permission.

Changing Symbol's Appearance

Quickly customizing how a symbol looks is another useful feature. By using the extensive symbol palette, users can quickly turn symbols into vibrant graphics. Follow these steps to change the appearance of a symbol.

1. Click one time on the symbol you would like to change.
2. Use the directional arrows on the symbol palette located to the left of the screen to navigate to an appropriate symbol library.

Figure 3.22: Symbol Palette

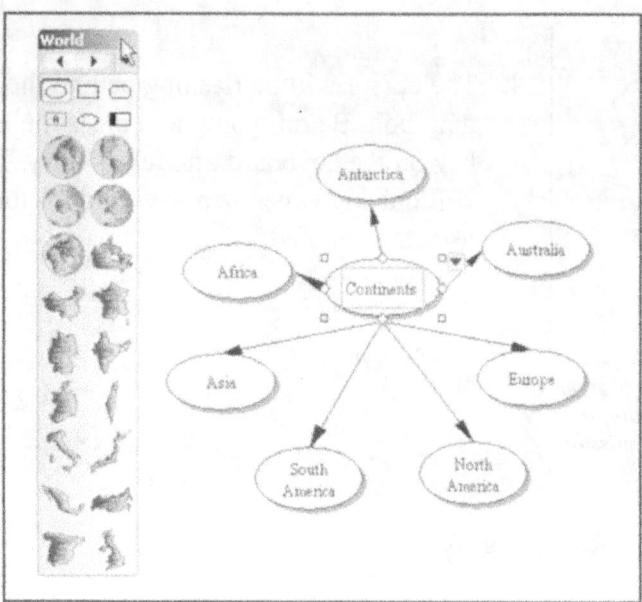

3. Placing the mouse pointer over a symbol will display a thumbnail preview of the graphic as well as provide a text description of the graphic in the bottom left hand corner of the screen.
4. Select the desired symbol by clicking on it. The symbol that was originally selected, in this case the Continents symbol, will now be replaced by the new symbol. In this example, all of the original symbols have been replaced by graphics.

This screen shot, created using Inspiration, published by Inspiration Software, Inc., is reprinted with permission.

Figure 3.23: Using Graphics

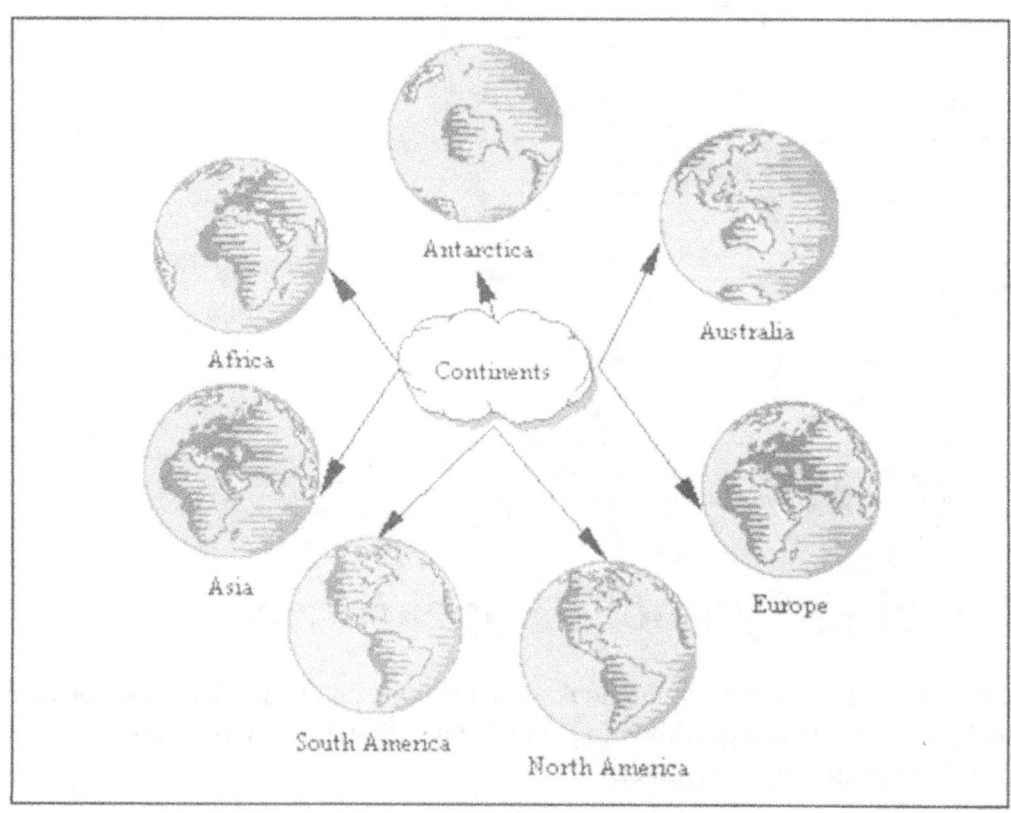

This screen shot, created using Inspiration, published by Inspiration Software, Inc., is reprinted with permission.

Opening a Template

As mentioned earlier, a very easy option for creating a thinking map or graphic organizer with Inspiration is to use the templates that come pre-loaded. Just follow these steps to begin working with templates.

1. Start the Inspiration program.
2. Click one time on the File menu and select Open Template.

Figure 3.24: Opening a Template

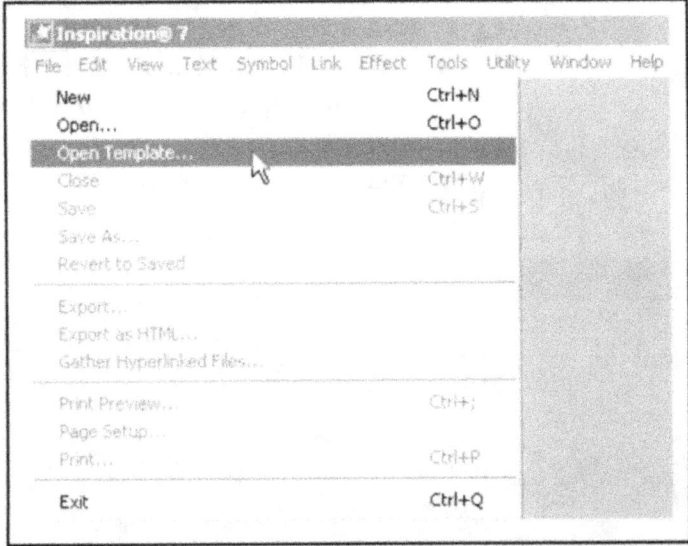

This screen shot, created using Inspiration, published by Inspiration Software, Inc., is reprinted with permission.

3. Select the desired template from the list provided.

Figure 3.25: Selecting a Template

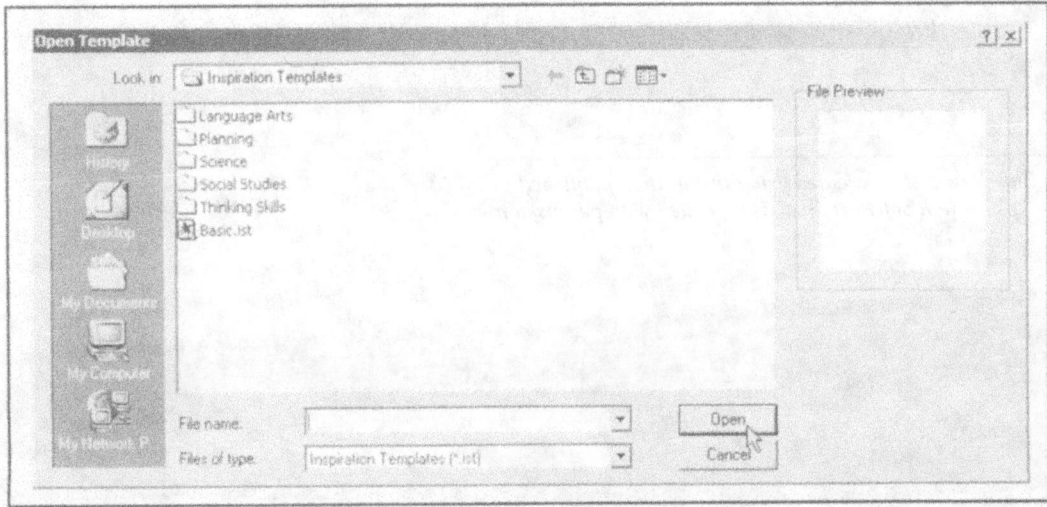

This screen shot, created using Inspiration, published by Inspiration Software, Inc., is reprinted with permission.

Saving a Custom Template

If you cannot locate a template to meet your needs, feel free to create and save your own by following these steps.

1. Create a diagram.
2. Click one time on the File menu and select Save As Template.

Figure 3.26: Saving a Diagram as a Template

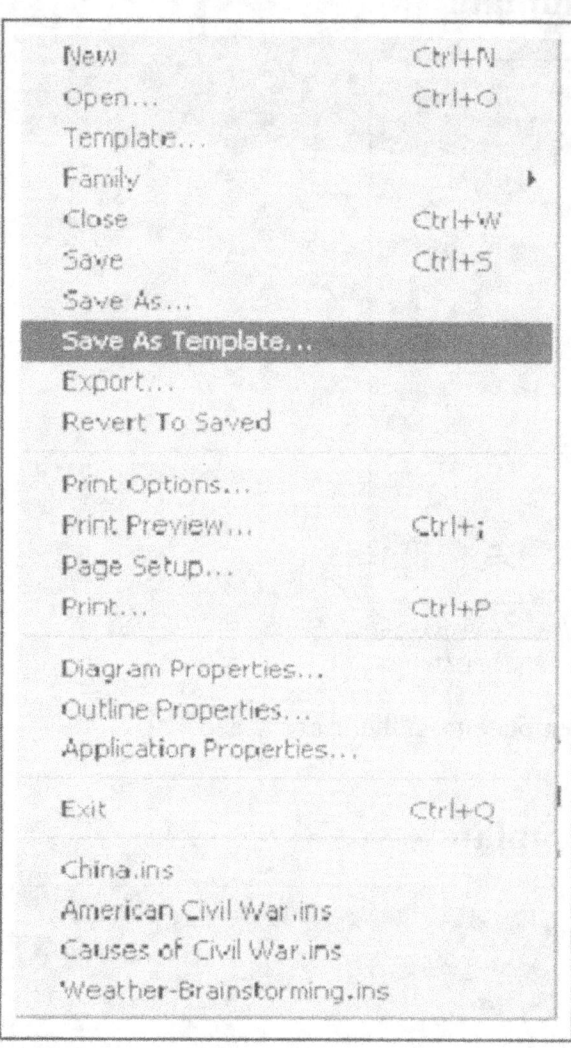

3. Name the template in the space provided.
4. To use the template in the future, simply click on the File menu, select Open Template, and open the desired template.

This screen shot, created using Inspiration, published by Inspiration Software, Inc., is reprinted with permission.

Notes on Using Kidspiration

While the focus of this chapter has been on Inspiration, Kidspiration, by the same developers, has been specifically designed for K–2 students. However, Kidspiration can be used with older elementary students as well. One feature that separates the two programs is the voice prompt that helps students select from different templates and menu items.

Figure 3.27: Kidspiration Opening Screen

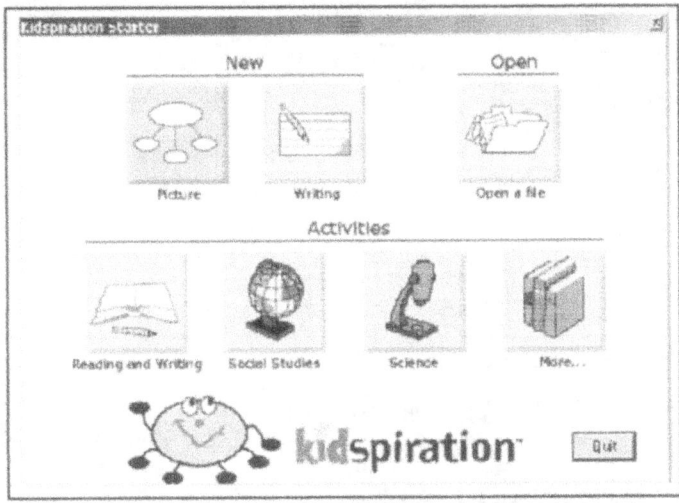

This screen shot, created using Kidspiration, published by Inspiration Software, Inc., is reprinted with permission.

Placing the mouse pointer over any of the items lights up the item and activates a voice prompt that identifies the item for the students.

After choosing an item, in this case the Picture icon, the starting screen shares some similarities with Inspiration, but the menu choices are simpler and easier for younger students to navigate and understand. As with the opening screen, placing the mouse pointer over any menu or toolbar item will activate a voice prompt identifying the item for the student.

Getting Started with a Kidspiration Diagram

Figure 3.28: Kidspiration Screen

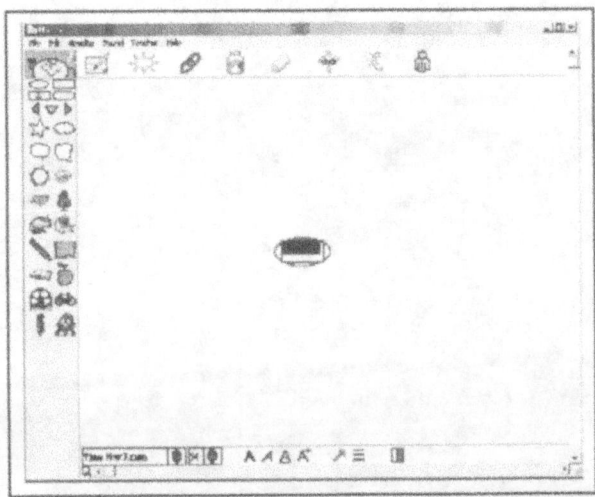

This screen shot, created using Kidspiration, published by Inspiration Software, Inc., is reprinted with permission.

Everything about the Kidspiration screen is designed with the young learner in mind. Font sizes and colors can easily be changed by clicking on the appropriate toolbar icon at the bottom of the window. Creating links and symbols is also simplified with bright, oversized buttons as well as voice prompts.

However, there is one truly unique feature that sets Kidspiration apart from its counterpart. The Listen feature enables students to listen to how a word is pronounced after it is typed on the screen. To use the Listen feature, do the following:

1. Create a symbol and type some text in it.
2. Click on the Listen icon (shaped like an ear) on the toolbar at the top of the screen.
3. As the student moves the mouse pointer back onto the diagram, the mouse pointer will take the shape of a tiny ear.
4. Click on the symbol and the program will "say" the word that is typed.

Figure 3.29: The Listen Button

This screen shot, created using Kidspiration, published by Inspiration Software, Inc., is reprinted with permission.

Examples Using Kidspiration

Figure 3.30: Characteristics of a Rabbit

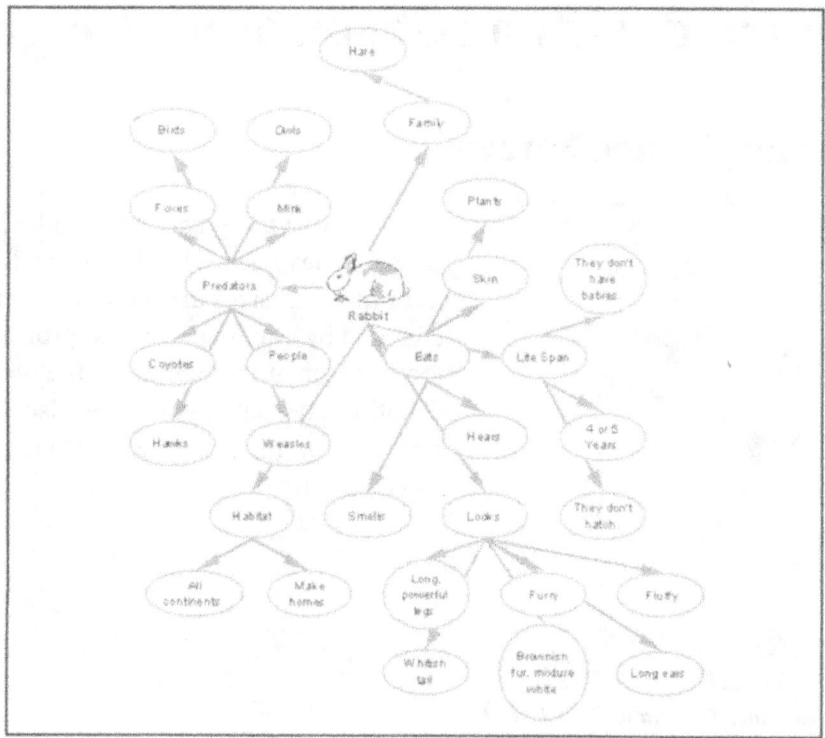

This screen shot, created using Kidspiration, published by Inspiration Software, Inc., is reprinted with permission.

Figure 3.31: A Profile of China

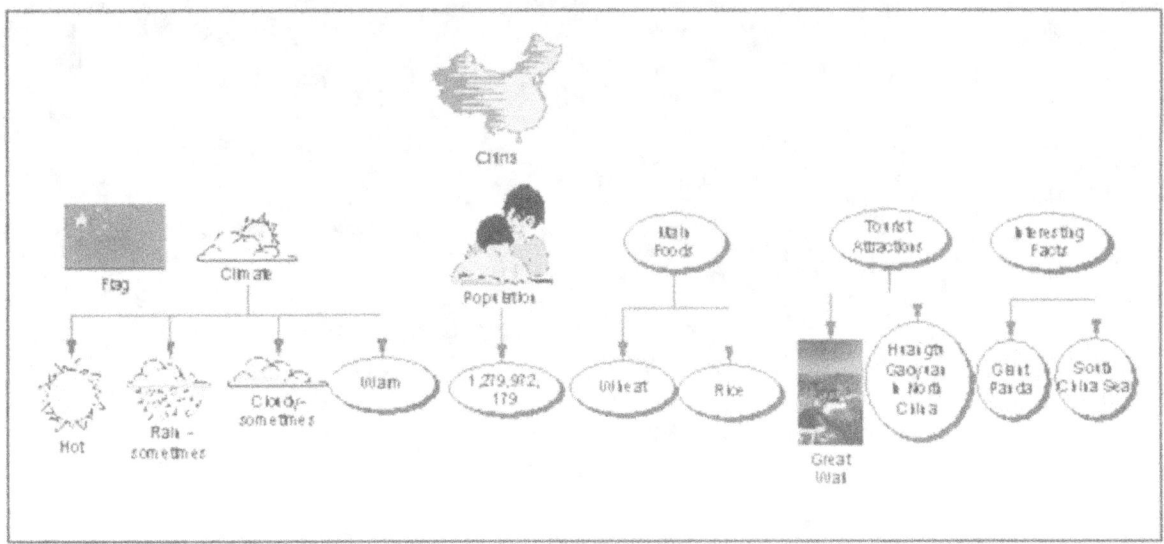

This screen shot, created using Kidspiration, published by Inspiration Software, Inc., is reprinted with permission.

Figure 3.32: An Aquarium Ecosystem

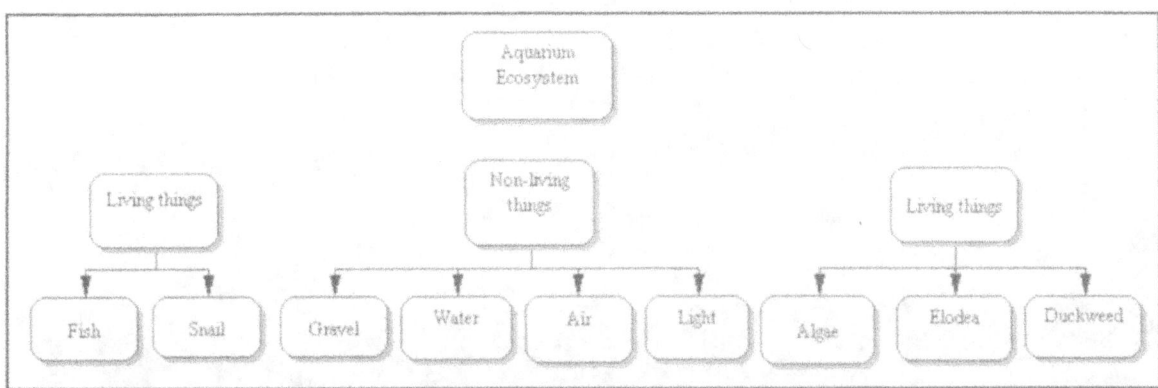

This screen shot, created using Kidspiration, published by Inspiration Software, Inc., is reprinted with permission.

Chapter 3: Thinking with Bubbles 53

Chapter 4

Assessment Tools to Improve Classroom Instruction

> *"Even if you're on the right track, you'll get run over if you just sit there."*
>
> —***Will Rogers***

All of us know that the best technology training focuses on integrating technology into the classroom. As trainers we hear, *"Make sure that it has to do with the academic standards."*

"Don't make the technology separate."
"Remember, teachers need to make sure that students pass state tests. Don't waste time."
"The material has to focus on higher order thinking skills. Don't focus on the little stuff."

But teachers come into technology classes with downtrodden looks. Some days are a struggle in the classroom. We hear teachers bemoan, *"We taught the students. We tested them. But... they flunked. What can we do?"*

Teachers have taught it, reviewed it, answered questions, and asked questions. What more can they do? What went wrong?

We suspect, maybe we even know, that the material they were trying to teach was too abstract and removed from the students' lives. After all, what relevance does the War of 1812 or *The Diary of Anne Frank* have when hormones are raging?

Or maybe the instruction was focused too much on knowledge that consisted of knowing dates, definitions, and major events. Did we connect the knowledge? Was the teaching **too remote, too repetitive**?

Maybe, just maybe, we went for the "big ideas" first. Maybe we cut to the chase and forgot to build the instruction on a solid base of knowledge. Higher order thinking needs to involve synthesis and analysis. So we went for it. State tests require that students think and use the knowledge. So why not focus on the problem-solving questions?

Or maybe we had another problem. Did we expect the students to learn largely through repetition and practice? Did we rely on the knowledge and skills presented by the textbook? Maybe, but, doggone, we had to do it.

So What Do We Know?

Students must learn by having basic knowledge. Integration of multiple kinds of knowledge and skills makes the collection of multiple sources of evidence over time and in different contexts necessary. Assessment is a developmental process that supports the academic standards. It provides a vehicle for self or peer assessment and opportunities for revision and refinement.

Our greatest challenge is to fashion a program of instruction that can adapt to the diversity in backgrounds, experiences, aspirations, and styles of learning that students bring to the classroom.

How Can We Do It?

There are wonderful tools on the Web that allow us to review, establish basic facts, and emphasize knowledge. In this chapter, we will look at one of the tools in depth. In this chapter, we will examine Hot Potatoes, a tool that allows us to create six different types of assessments. We focus on this because Hot Potatoes <http://web.uvic.ca/hrd/hotpot/> has no pop-up advertisements or banner ads. In fact, since the program is downloaded directly to your computer, you have complete control over the content. Once the program is downloaded, the user may generate Web pages with interactive quizzes. These Web pages may then be uploaded to the teacher's own Web site.

Available from the University of Victoria, the Hot Potatoes suite is free of charge for non-profit, educational users who post examples on the Web. All other users must pay a license fee.

Hot Potatoes

One of Hot Potatoes biggest attractions is that it does not require a lot of technical knowledge. If you are able to navigate on the Web and follow directions, you can handle Hot Potatoes. Only one download is required; after that Hot Potatoes runs from your own PC or Mac. No knowledge of programming or HTML is necessary (Hallelujah!).

Students, attracted to the interactive quizzes created from Hot Potatoes, generally enjoy the Web-based exercises. The exercises may be accessed from a Web site that the teacher has created or may be easily accessed by students at any computer with a standard Web browser.

Students take the quizzes and correct their own work based on the clues and feedback set up in advance by the teacher. It is not even necessary to have an Internet connection.

Even though the quizzes you make with Hot Potatoes take the form of HTML (Web pages), you do not need to know HTML and there is no need to post the quizzes to the Web for them to work correctly. After Hot Potatoes generates the necessary HTML files for you, the teacher can have the students run the pages from the hard drive if necessary.

With accountability, there's a heavy emphasis on content. As teachers, we all want to get to problem-solving questions—to watch students learn to apply the knowledge. In quality assessment, different levels of thinking have to be going on. Hot Potatoes allows that to happen.

The Six Applications

The flexibility that Hot Potatoes offers is one of its greatest features. Quick scans of student learning—informal assessments—are key hallmarks of Hot Potatoes. Even with the multiple-choice format, the teacher can select multiple answers to be correct (shades of the bane of many students' existence—*all of the above*). Students enjoy the quick check of knowledge. In the Web page format, users move the answers around. Using a drag-and-drop format, students select answers and get immediate feedback.

Six different applications are available. With Hot Potatoes, teachers can create Web-based online quizzes using **multiple,choice, short-answer, jumbled-sentence, crossword, matching,** and **fill-in-the-blank exercises**. These easy to produce quizzes, saved as HTML and placed on your own Web page, are a real draw for students.

One Potato, JCloze, produces gaps. Whether the teacher wishes to demonstrate to students the relationship of word and meaning or to create a fill-in-the blank or short-answer test, it can be accomplished quickly. To create a gap-filled exercise, click on a word and then onto **Gap** or click on **Autogap** (Autogap selects the places for gaps to occur).

Two Potato is JCross, the crossword puzzle maker. Simply type words onto a grid. After producing a crossword, add your clues. An example of a crossword puzzle on insects is available at <http://www.highland.madison.k12.il.us/teacher/mscholl/insectcrossword.htm>.

Figure 4.1: Crossword Puzzle

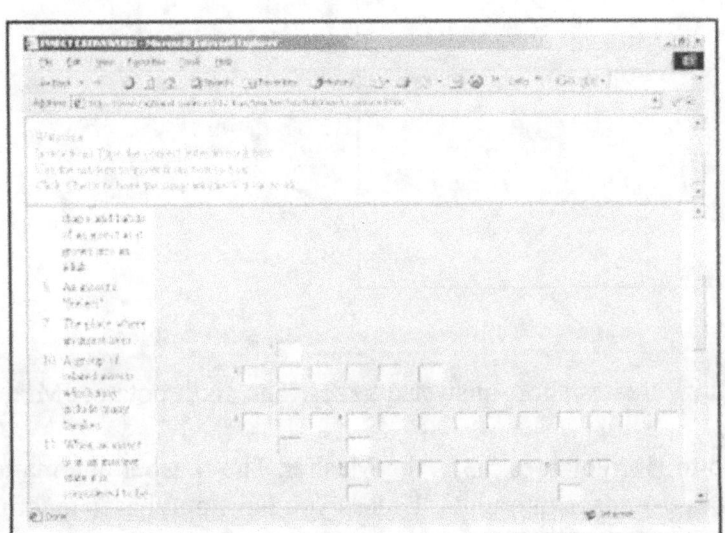

Three Potato is JBC, a multiple-choice program. Enter your questions (as many as you like) and then enter the correct answer and as many other choices as you wish. Once the items are checked, the default for a right or wrong answer is a smiley face or an X. An example of this format is a quiz on the U.S. Constitution available at <http://www.highland.madison.k12.il.us/teacher/tfunderburk/practice_test.htm>.

Figure 4.2: Multiple-Choice Quiz

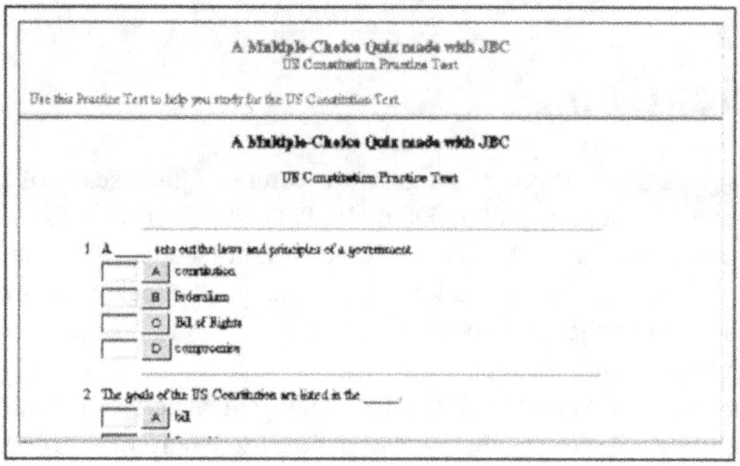

Four Potato is JMatch, a matching test module. As with all of the other potatoes, pictures and audio may be added to the format. A quiz on lab equipment is available online at <http://www.highland.madison.k12.il.us/teacher/lbasden/equipquiz.htm>.

Figure 4.3: Lab Equipment

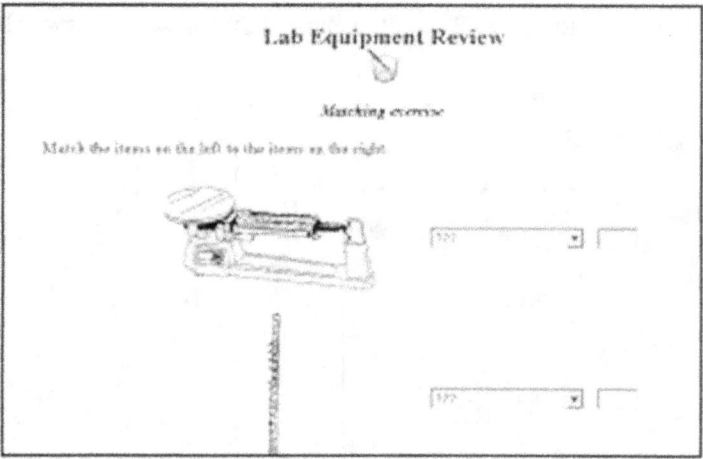

The fifth potato, JQuiz, creates short-answer quizzes. The sixth potato, JMix, creates a jumbled-sentence exercise.

A new feature added to Hot Potatoes 5.3 is the Masher. The Masher automatically compiles various Hot Potatoes exercises into units. Unless you have purchased a commercial license for Hot Potatoes, you may combine only three exercises with the Masher.

Applications Are Easy to Use

The Hot Potato applications are easy to use. Most importantly, students like them. For students, the attractiveness of the interactive Web environment and the auto-correct feature are compelling.

Strengths of Hot Potatoes

The strengths of Hot Potatoes are many. With the software, it is relatively simple to:

- include timed reading texts;
- create timed tests;
- include hypertext links;
- include images and audio and video files;
- and create multiple-choice tests and matching, short-answer, scrambled word or sentence exercises, crossword puzzles, and fill-in-the-blank activities.

Exhibit Center

Examples of Assessment Materials on the Web

The following examples illustrate the various uses of the assessment materials available on the Web.

With Hot Potatoes, quick-take tests on terms can be constructed by offering a new version of the multiple-choice test. With the drop down boxes, students can click on the best answer.

Figure 4.4: Review of Poetry Terms

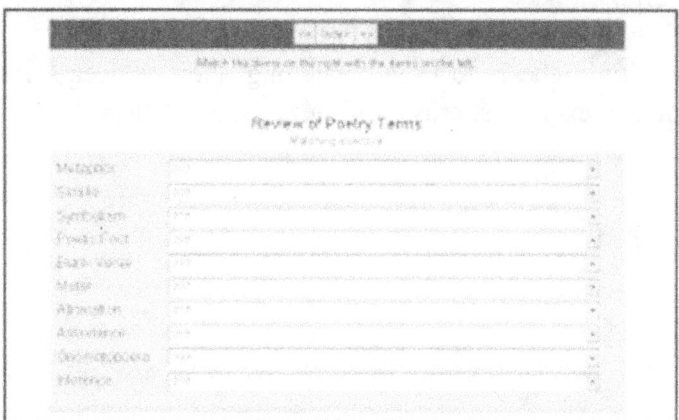

Another example allows us to incorporate a reading text. The reading text may be keyed in, or it may be copied and pasted from the Web or another document. The neat part about this example is that the sample test is set up similar to many states' reading comprehension sections. This allows students to become familiar with the format and also encourages close reading of the text. In this particular example, there is a series of 11 questions on the text. The complete example of this test may be found at <http://www.spa3.k12.sc.us/annabell.htm>.

Figure 4.5: A Journey Through Poe

The previous example is part of a guided tour (see the authors' previous book, *Web-based Learning: A Practical Guide*, Linworth, 2001). You may also wish to explore the Guided Tour available at <http://www.spa3.k12.sc.us/WebQuests/Poe/poe.html>. The Poe Guided Tour demonstrates the extensive use a teacher can get out of the quick assessments. The assessments range from a review of biographical information to a quiz on understanding poetry. The assessments cover a range from knowledge to application.

Figure 4.6: Poe's "Annabel Lee"

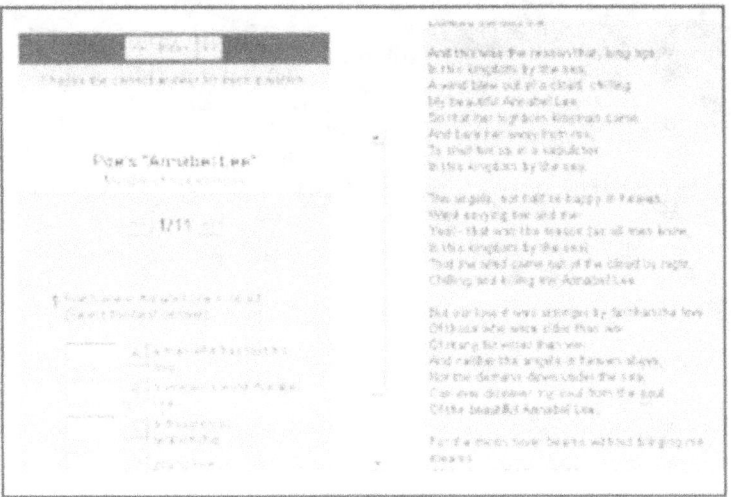

In Figure 4.7, Hot Potatoes is used to give us a quick assessment of Edgar Allan Poe's life. Relying on quick facts, the teacher developed the test to review some basic information that students should know. This example is structured in a standard, multiple-choice format. Notice that near the top of the assessment a running percentage of correct items will be maintained. That is one of the things that students appear to enjoy most: immediate feedback. Particularly in cases where you are checking on factual recall, it is useful for students to know immediately if they know the material. The format of this test is also friendly enough to students that they will be more apt to review for a unit test with the quizzes.

Figure 4.7: Poe's Biographical Information

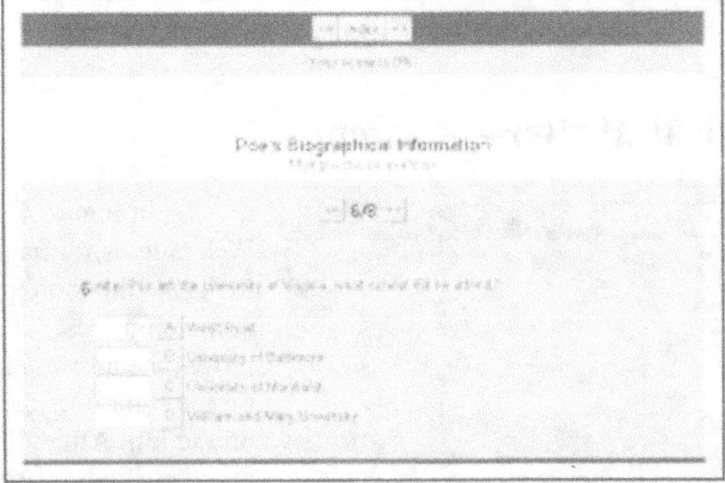

In Figure 4.8, the feedback option is used. The feedback option in the Hot Potatoes example allows the teacher to add additional information to the quiz. Notice that in Figure 4.8, if students select Robert Frost (a wrong answer), they will receive feedback in the form of a text message that "Robert Frost is most famous for his poetry."

Figure 4.8: American Writers

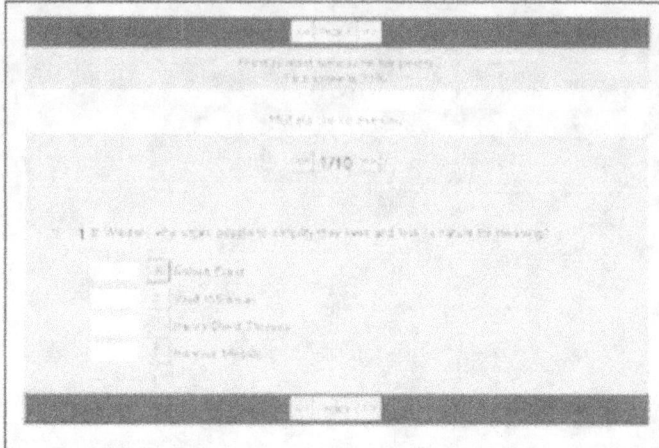

In the next example, Figure 4.9, we have added text.

Figure 4.9: The "I Have a Dream" Speech

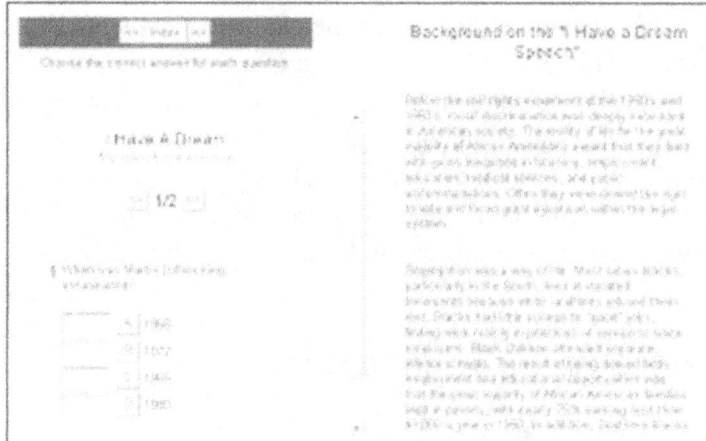

In Figure 4.10, the test has been generated by having a student click on a drop down menu of names. If a student gets some answers incorrect, the items that were incorrect will disappear when he or she clicks Check.

Figure 4.10: American Writers—Matching

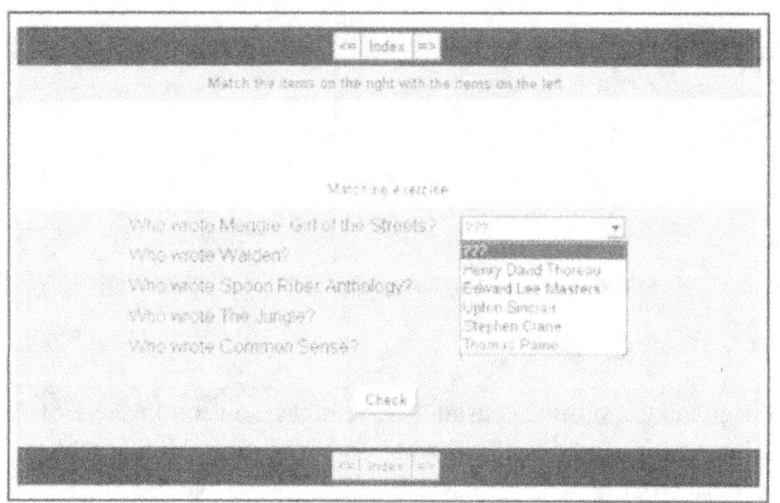

In Figure 4.11, the Web page is formatted to look like the more traditional matching test. The student moves the answers located on the right over the items on the left. After all items are identified, the student clicks Check. Those items that are incorrect return to the right hand column. Those items that are correct stay to the left.

62 Technology Timesavers: Simple Steps to Increasing Classroom Productivity

Figure 4.11: American Writers Series

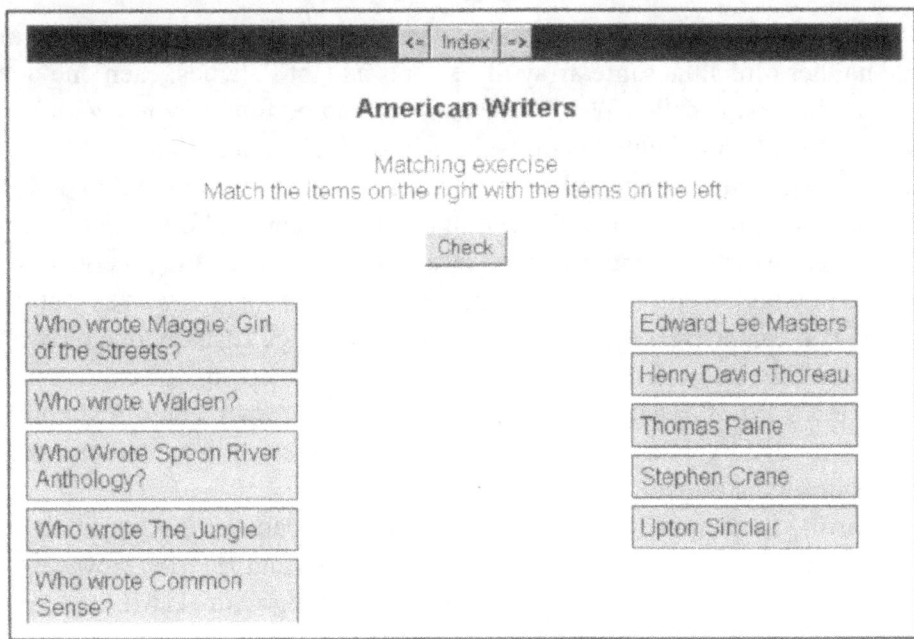

This is an example of a mixed-up word sentence. Mixed-up word sentences are one way to teach the order and structure of the English language. In this example, there are several correct possibilities. All of these possibilities can be added to the menu of correct responses.

Figure 4.12: Mixed-Up Sentence

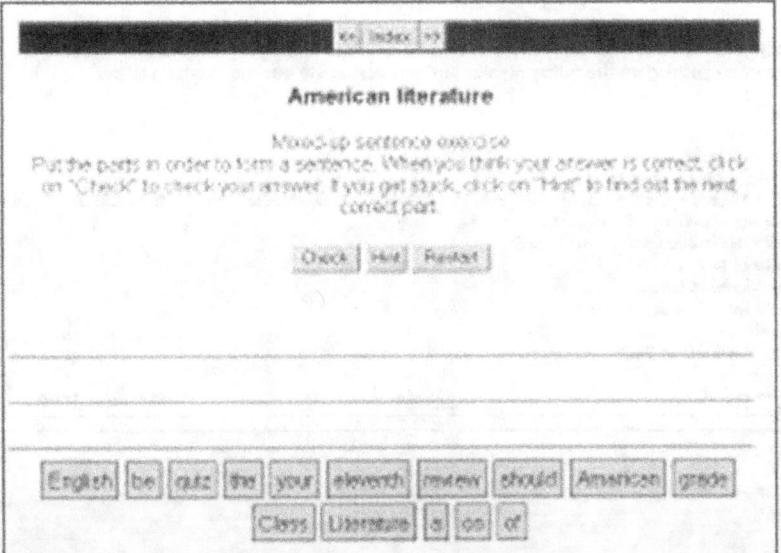

Other Interactive Exercise Makers

There are at least two other free online interactive exercise makers worth including in this chapter. While neither offers the same array of features as Hot Potatoes, each one does have unique strengths. The first is called WebPractest, which can be found by navigating to <http://www.wm.edu/CAS/modlang/gasmit/webpractest/>. The main feature of this free service is that it allows you to create fill-in-the-blanks from the existing text in a Web page. In other words, let's say you have created a test in a word processor. You wish to create fill-in-the-blank spaces in which students can type in the correct answer and receive immediate feedback indicated by both a color-coded system of right or wrong answers as well as a numeric score. If you can convert the document into a Web page (usually one or two fairly simple steps), it can then be used in a WebPractest exercise. Once you have a test in Web page format, there is a set of directions provided at <http://www.wm.edu/CAS/modlang/gasmit/webpractest/> that explains how to convert this document into an exercise containing fill-in-the-blanks designed by you.

If it is starting to sound a little complicated, that is because it is. One really needs to have a good understanding of creating and editing Web pages and HTML. However, there is a payoff. For those who are proficient and comfortable working with HTML and Web pages, WebPractest enables you to continue to use fully functional Web pages that you have created with all of the original formatting, images, and layout. It allows you to take any Web page and to convert as much of it as you want into fill-in-the-blank sentences. Below is an example of a Guided Tour on Edgar Allan Poe after WebPractest converted it.

Figure 4.13: WebPractest Exercise

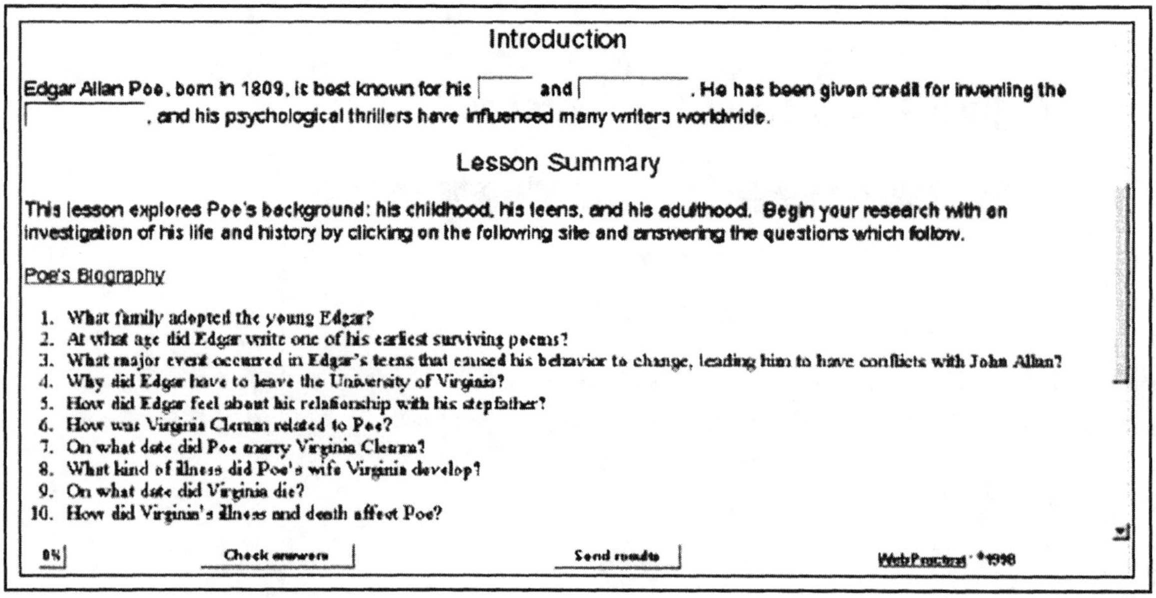

Interactive Exercise Makers

The second alternative to Hot Potatoes is a group of online Interactive Exercise Makers produced by Dan Beeby and the Tricollege Mellon Language Project at Haverford, Bryn Mawr, and Swarthmore colleges. The tools provided at <http://makers.cet.middlebury.edu/makers/index.htm> include:

- **DictoMaker**—enables students to highlight a word in the body of a text and do a dictionary search on it;
- **ClozeMaker**—creates online fill-in-the-blank quizzes;
- **EvalMaker**—lets you type a question and provides a textbox for a student response and also provides a space for the teacher's answer (the student can click a button to compare the two responses);
- **MatchMaker**—creates a matching quiz;
- **MultiMaker**—creates a multiple-choice quiz; and
- **DHTML (Dynamic HTML) Makers**—creates activities where a student may drag-and-drop the various elements on a quiz.

The appeal of the Interactive Exercise Makers is that the developers have created easy-to-follow forms to help you create the activities. The forms allow you to copy and paste existing text to make the quizzes.

Once the information on the form has been entered, the activity is automatically saved to the Web and given a URL. The developers recommend saving the activity to your local hard drive and to post the exercises on your own or your school's Web site. This diagram, provided at the Web site, explains the process clearly.

Figure 4.14: Interactive Exercise Maker at Swarthmore College

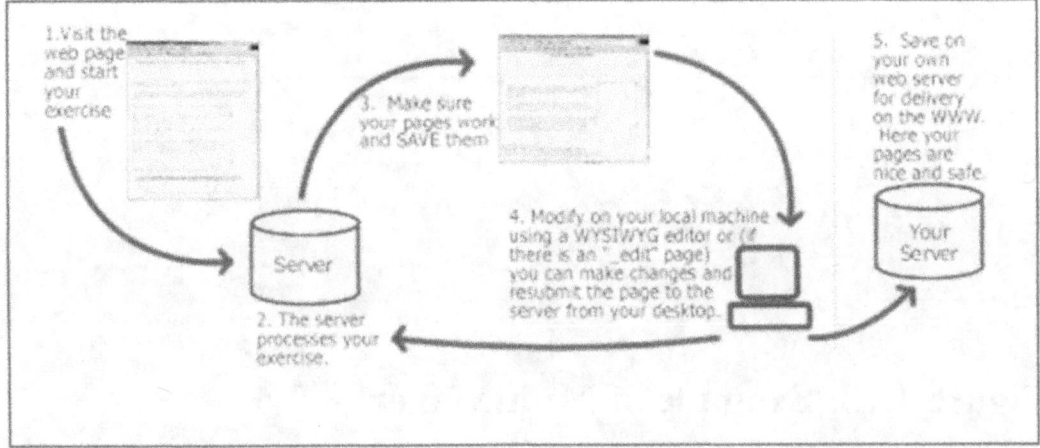

Figure 4.15: Example of Clozemaker

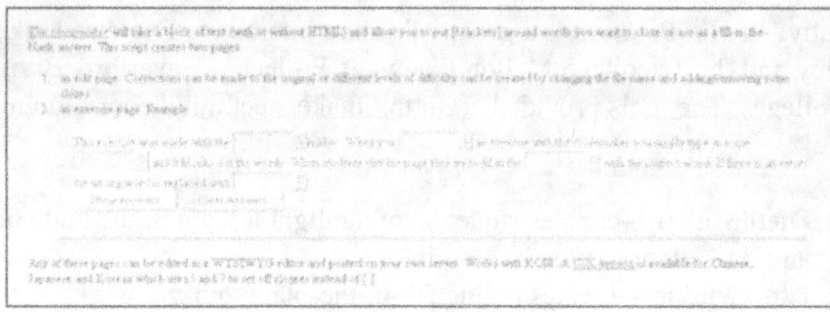

Figure 4.16: Example of EvalMaker

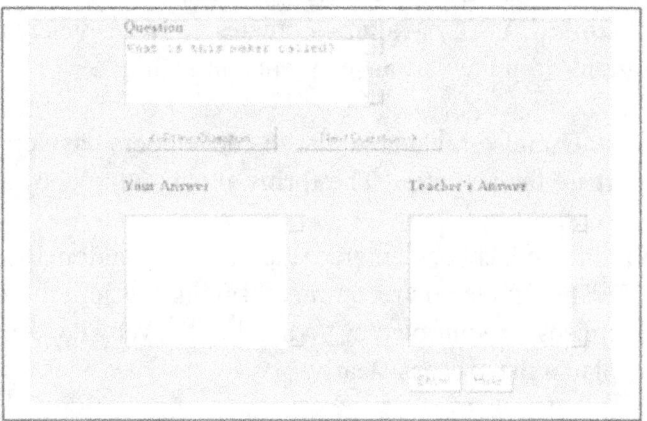

Figure 4.17: Example of MatchMaker

Figure 4.18: Example of MultiMaker

Show Me How It's Done

This section covers the basic steps required to use Hot Potatoes.

Getting Started

Downloading Hot Potatoes <http://web.uvic.ca/hrd/hotpot/>:

1. Copy the URL to Hot Potatoes homepage.
2. Navigate to the Download section.

Figure 4.19: Hot Potatoes Homepage

3. Click on the first bullet to download a self-extracting file.

Figure 4.20: Downloads

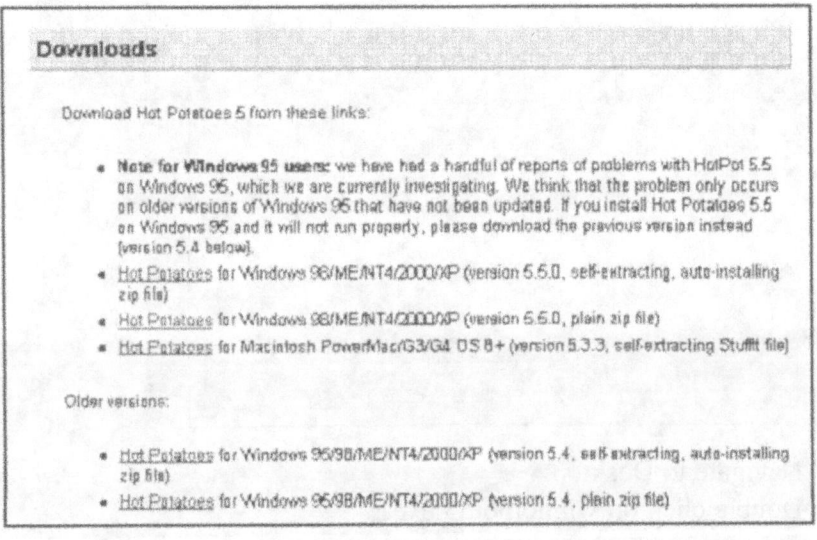

4. Check the box Save this program to disk.
5. Click OK.

Chapter 4: Assessment Tools to Improve Classroom Instruction 67

Figure 4.21: File Download

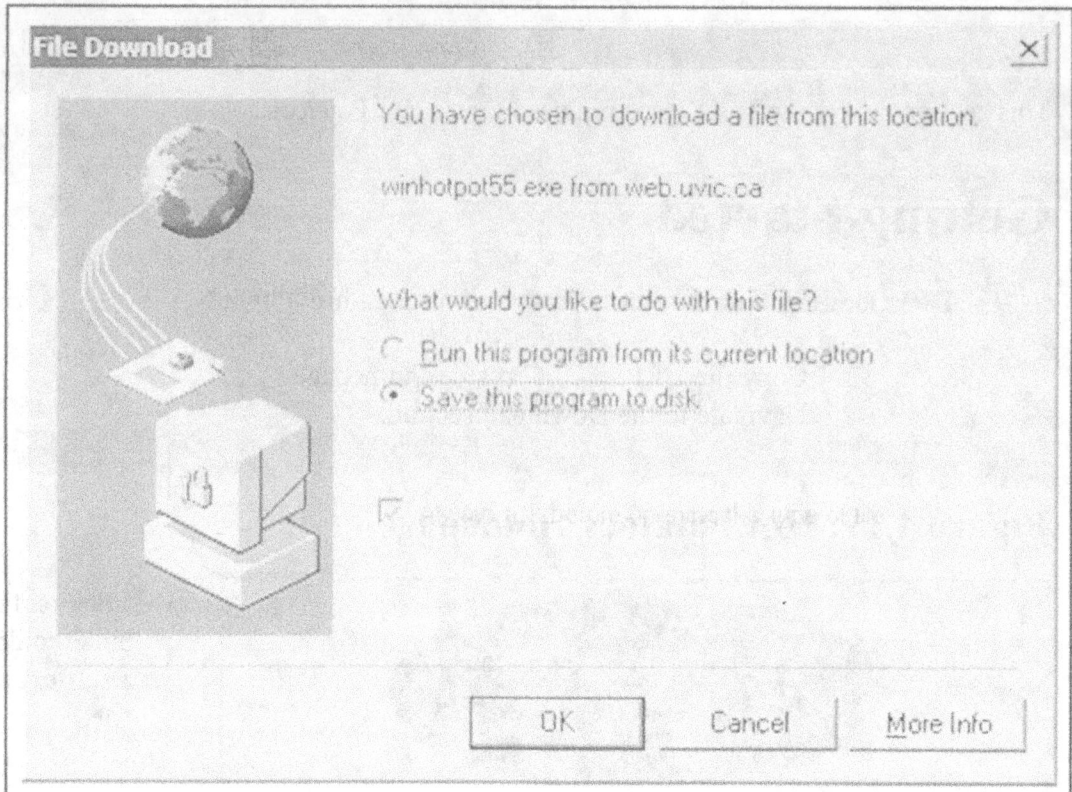

6. Navigate to Desktop.
7. Click Save.

Figure 4.22: Save As

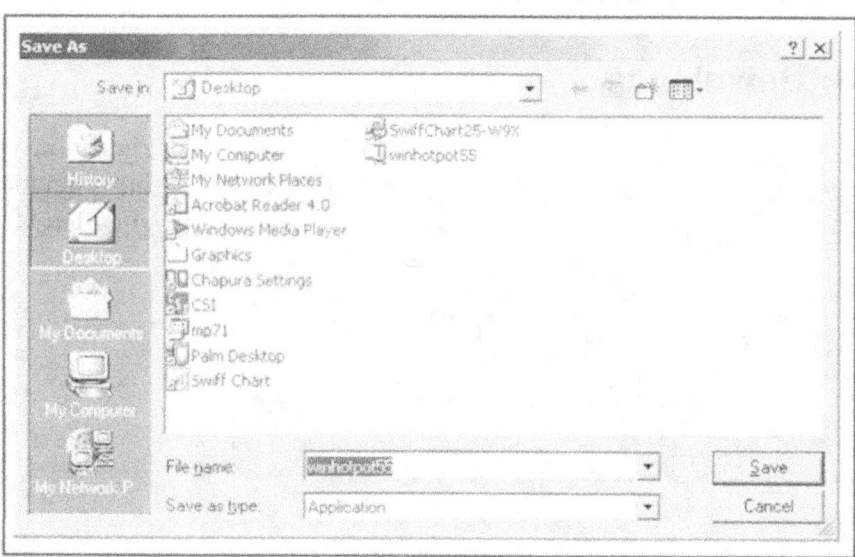

8. Navigate to Desktop.
9. Double click on winhotpot55.exe.

Figure 4.23: Desktop

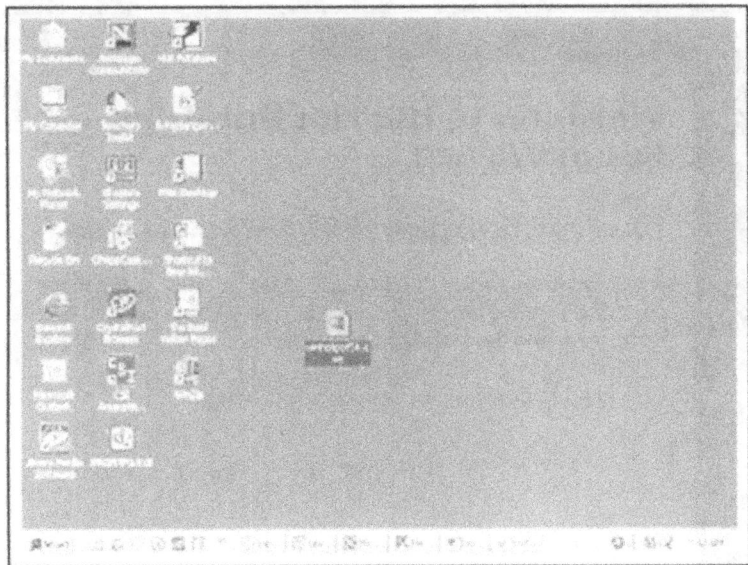

10. Click on Setup.

Figure 4.24: Self-Extractor

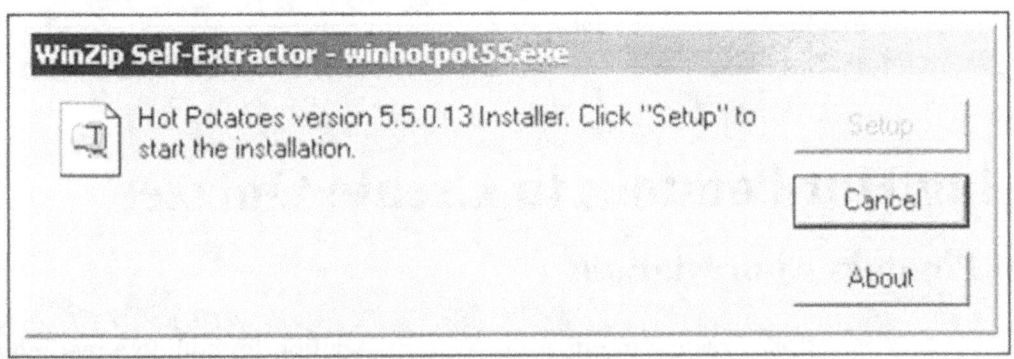

11. Click Yes.

Figure 4.25: Setup

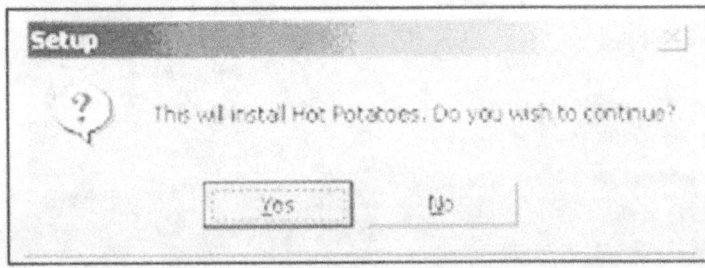

12. Click Next until Hot Potatoes is installed.

Figure 4.26: Setup Wizard

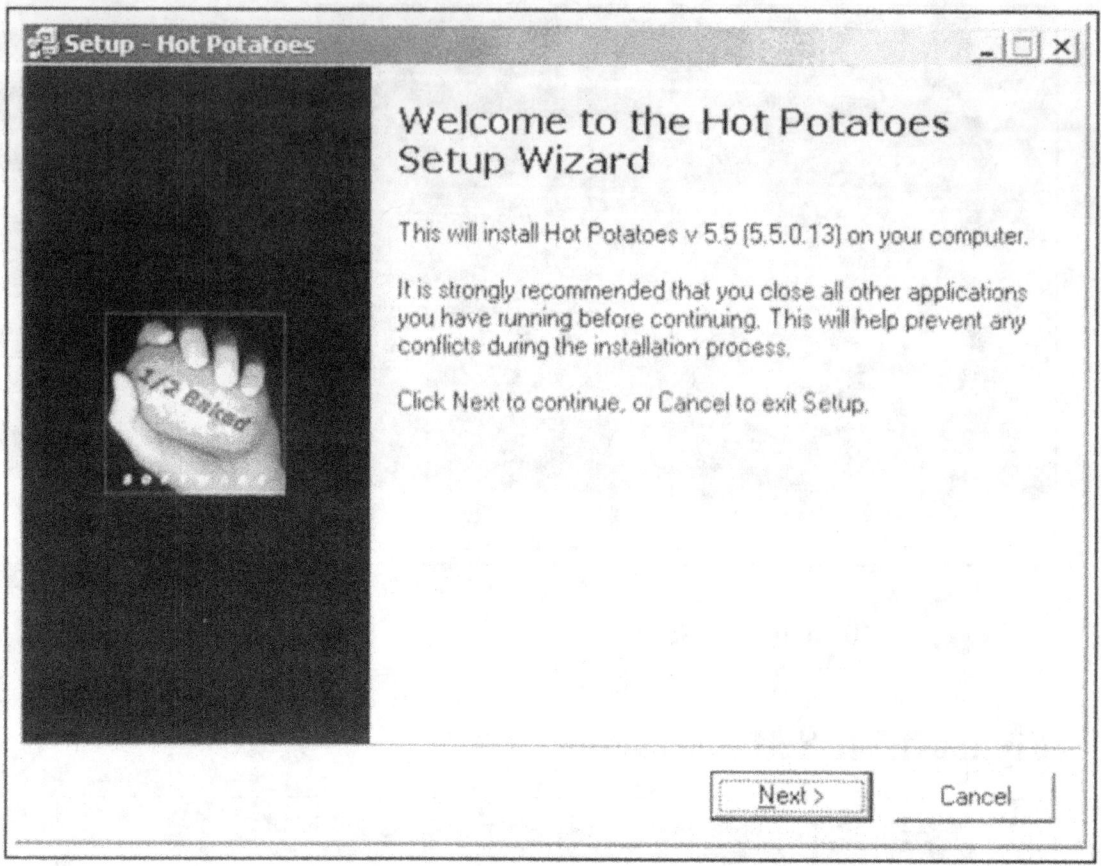

Using Hot Potatoes to Create Quizzes

Hot Potatoes Abbreviations

- JBC: Create a multiple-choice quiz—option for adding a reading text
- JQuiz: Create a short-answer quiz
- JMix: Create a jumbled-sentence exercise
- JCross: Create a crossword puzzle
- JMatch: Create a matching exercise
- JCloze: Create a fill-in-the-blank exercise

First Steps—Starting Hot Potatoes

1. Click on the short cut that has been created on your desktop.

Figure 4.27: Hot Potatoes Short Cut

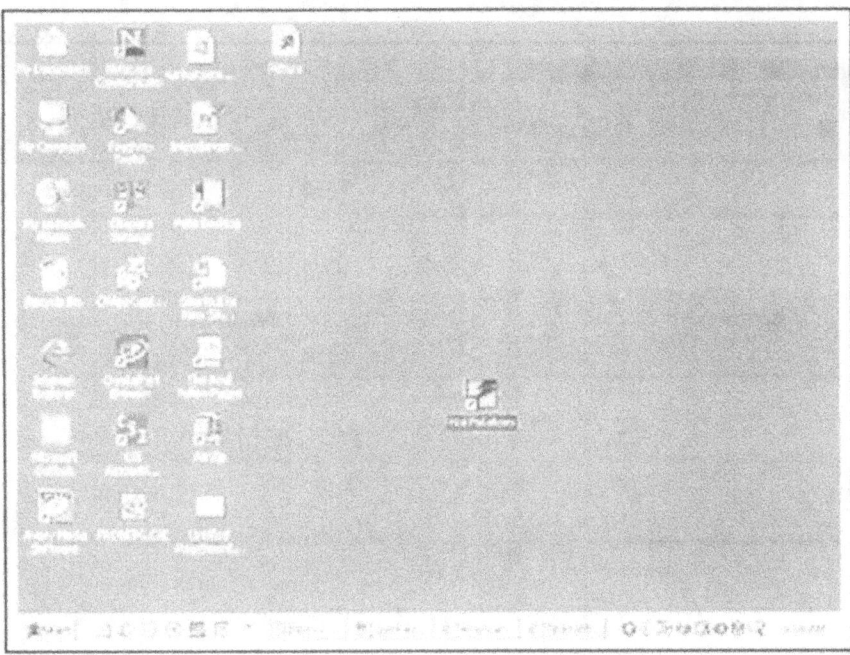

2. Click on the Potato (JBC, etc.) that you wish to open.

Figure 4.28: Click on Potato

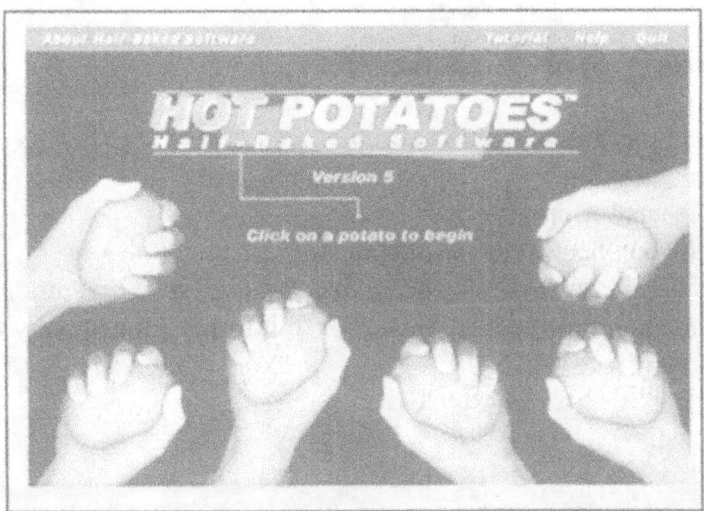

Using JBC

3. Click on JBC. The screen will appear formatted for multiple-choice questions.

Figure 4.29: JBC Screen

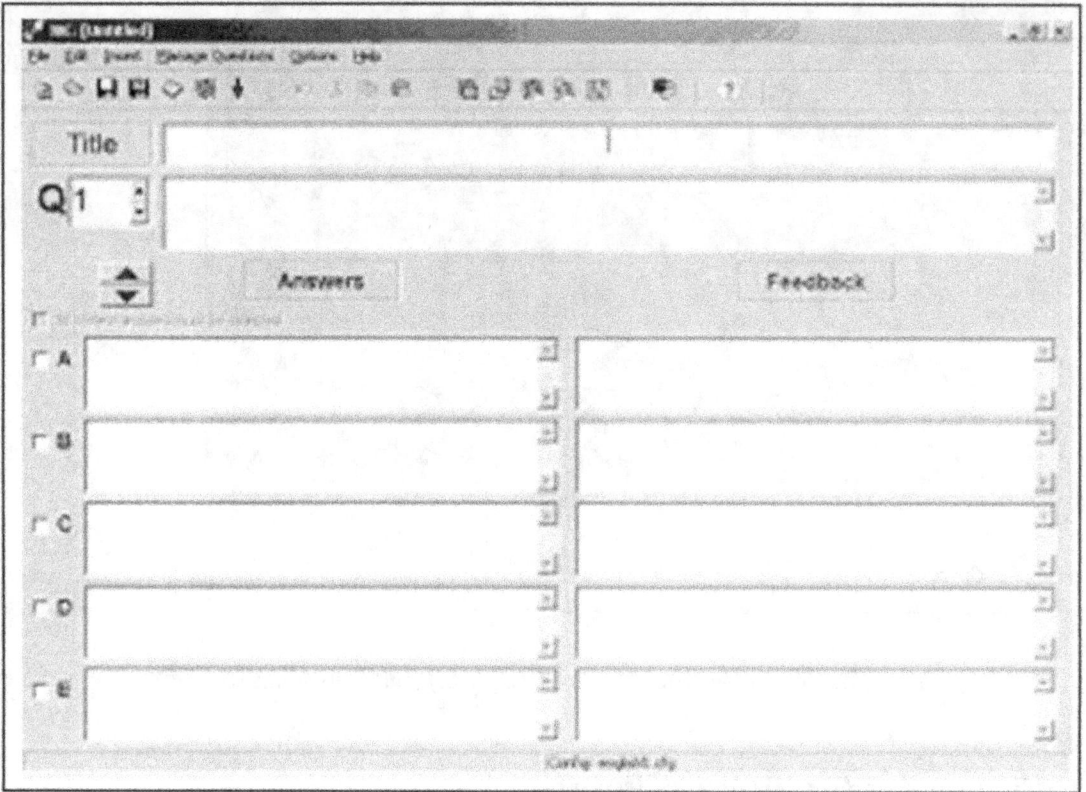

Steps to Creating an Exercise

4. Type in the title of your test.
5. Type in the question.
6. Type in the answer options.
7. Click in the box next to the correct answer.
8. Add feedback if you wish. Feedback may be used to add additional information about the correct answer or to inform a student why the answer is incorrect.

Adding text

(These are the same steps that you would take to add text for any of the Hot Potatoes):

9. If you wish to add text to the exercise, click on File.
10. Click on Add Reading Text.

Figure 4.30: Add Text

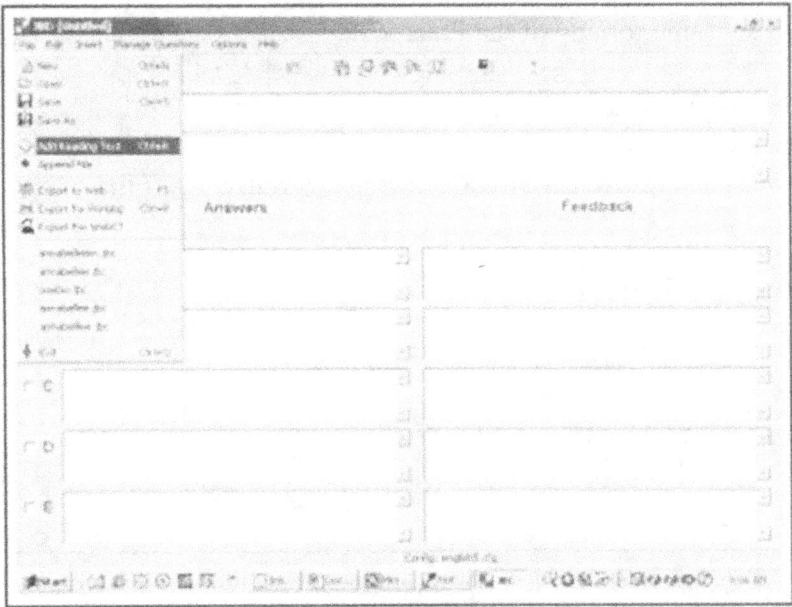

Adding Reading Text

Figure 4.31: Dialogue Box

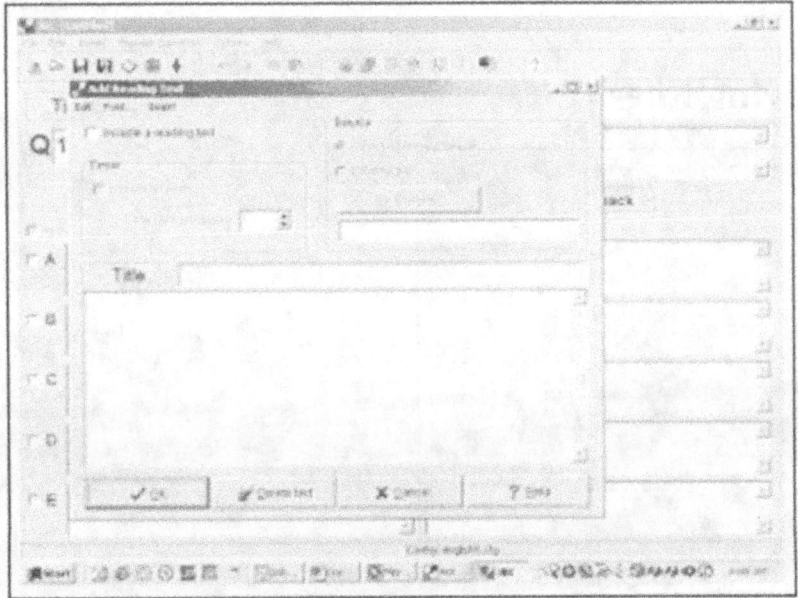

Chapter 4: Assessment Tools to Improve Classroom Instruction 73

11. Click in the left-hand box. Include a reading text.
12. Key in the title of the text.
13. Paste or key in the desired reading text.
14. Click OK.
15. Reading text will now be added to your multiple-choice test.

Inserting a Picture

(These instructions are the same for any of the Potatoes):

16. Click on the Insert Menu.
17. Click on Picture.
18. Select Picture from Web URL or Picture from Local File.

Figure 4.32: Insert Picture

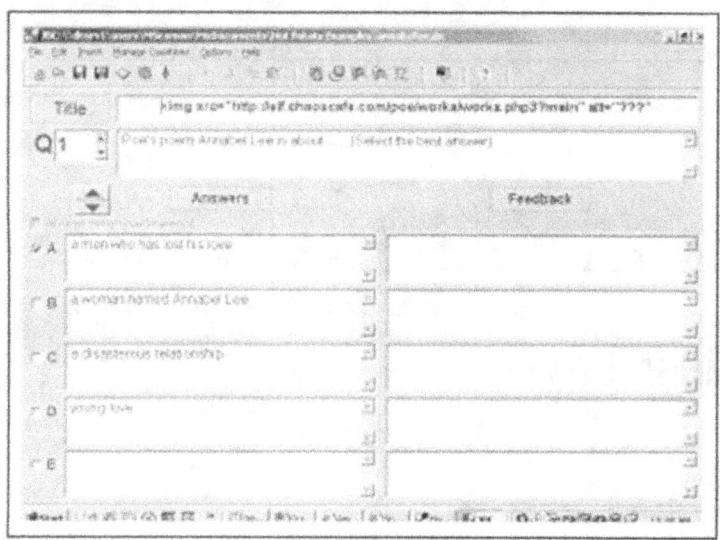

Figure 4.33: Saving Files

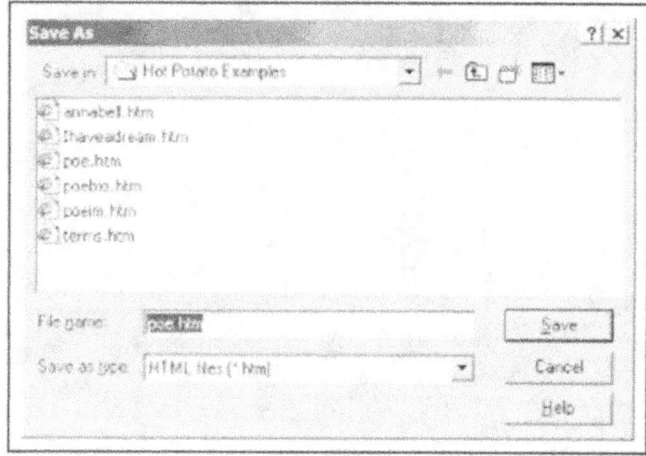

Saving Your Files

(These instructions are the same for any of the Potatoes):

19. Click on Web icon.
20. A Save As window will open.
21. Name your file and click Save. An information box will pop-up.
22. To preview your file, click Yes.

Figure 4.34: Information Box

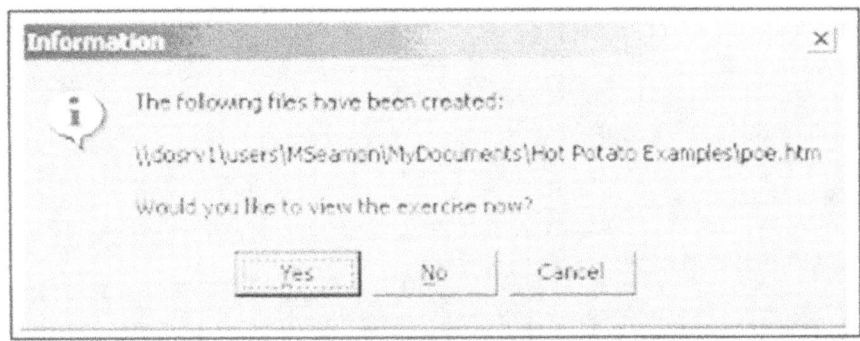

23. Your file will appear as a Web page.

Figure 4.35: Web Page File

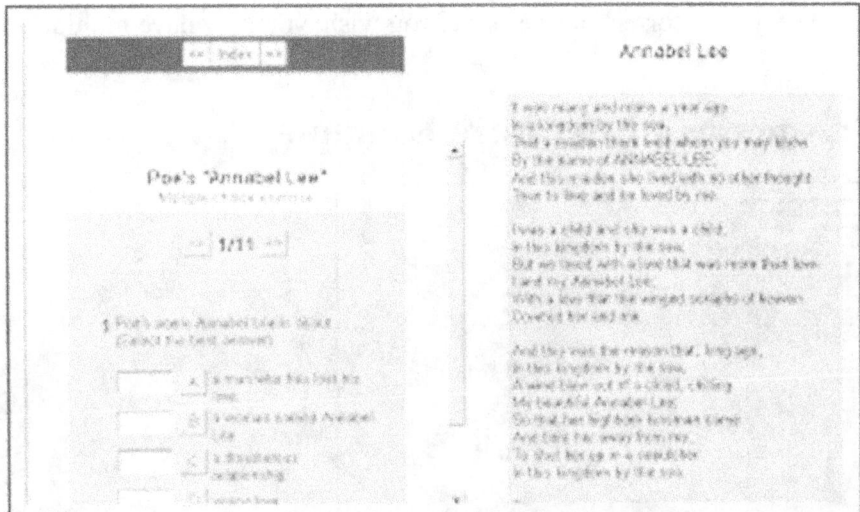

Chapter 4: Assessment Tools to Improve Classroom Instruction 75

Using JQuiz

1. Click on JQuiz. The screen will appear formatted for a short-answer quiz.

Figure 4.36: JQuiz

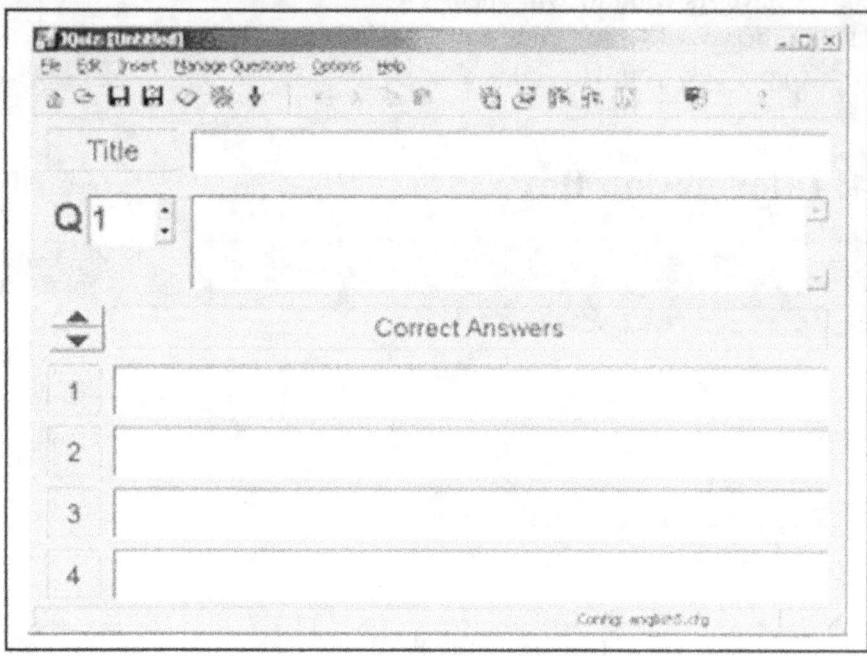

2. Key in the title of the test.
3. Key in the first question.
4. Key in the correct answer(s). If you wish, you may have multiple answers.

Figure 4.37: American Literature Example

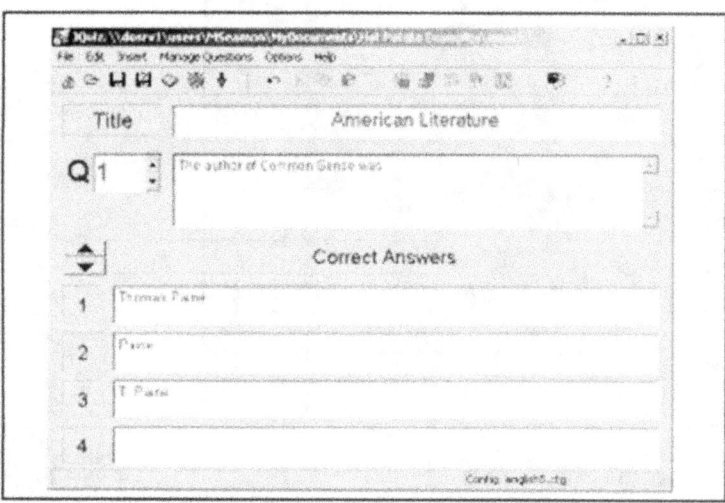

5. Click on the up arrow in the Q box to add additional questions.

Using JMix

1. Click on JMix. The screen will appear formatted for a jumbled-sentence exercise.

Figure 4.38: JMix

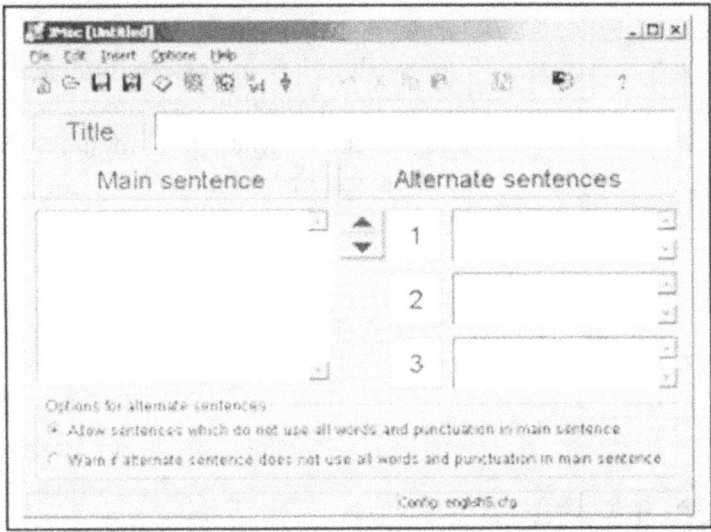

2. Add Title.
3. Key in Main sentence.
4. Key in Alternate sentences if appropriate (these would be considered acceptable answers).

Figure 4.39: JMix Example

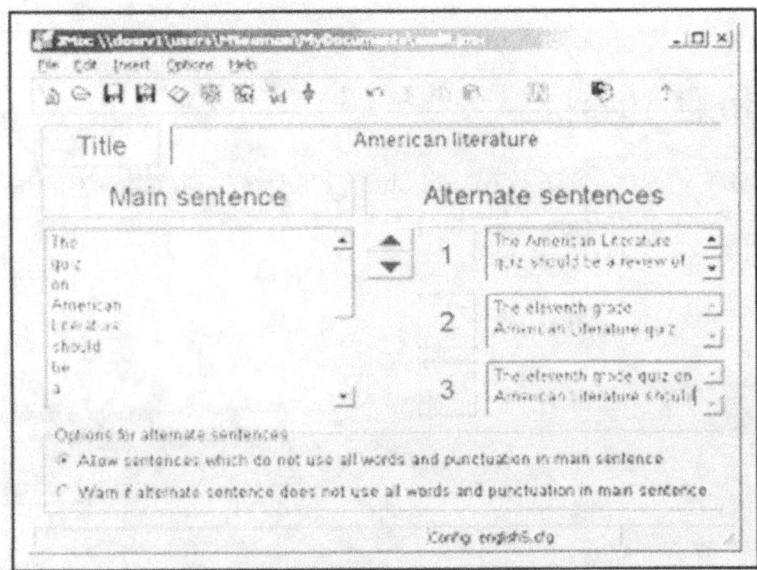

Chapter 4: Assessment Tools to Improve Classroom Instruction 77

Using JCross

1. Click on JCross. The screen will appear formatted for a crossword puzzle.

Figure 4.40: JCross

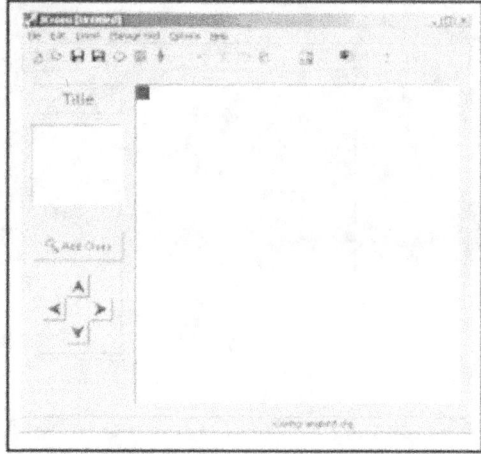

2. If you wish to make your own grid, type one letter in each crossword block.
3. If you wish to key in answers only and have the grid automatically generated, click on the menu bar choice Manage Grid and then click on Automatic grid-maker.

Figure 4.41: Crossword Grid

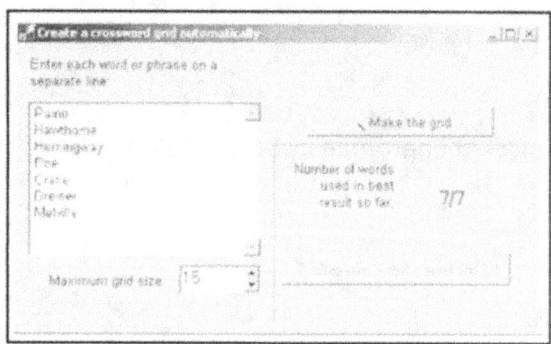

4. A new screen will pop up. Key each answer into the box, placing each word or phrase on a separate line.
5. After you have entered the answers, click on Make the grid.

Figure 4.42: Adding Clues

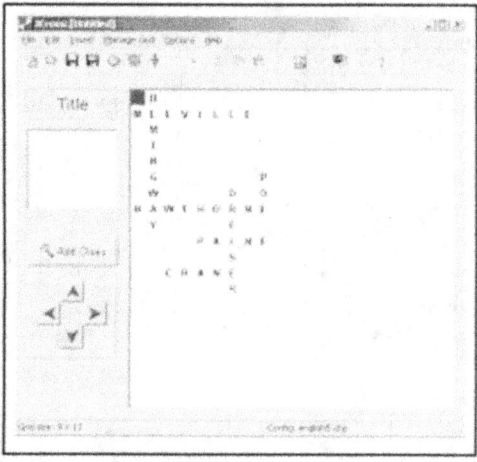

6. To add clues, click on Add Clues (to the left of screen).

Using JMatch

1. Click on JMatch. The screen will appear formatted for a matching exercise.
2. Key in the title of the test.
3. Key in Items that will be matched by the right column. These items will stay in the order in which they are keyed.
4. Key in answers in the correct order in the right column. Unless you check the Fix column to the right of the answers, they will be jumbled automatically.

Figure 4.43: JMatch

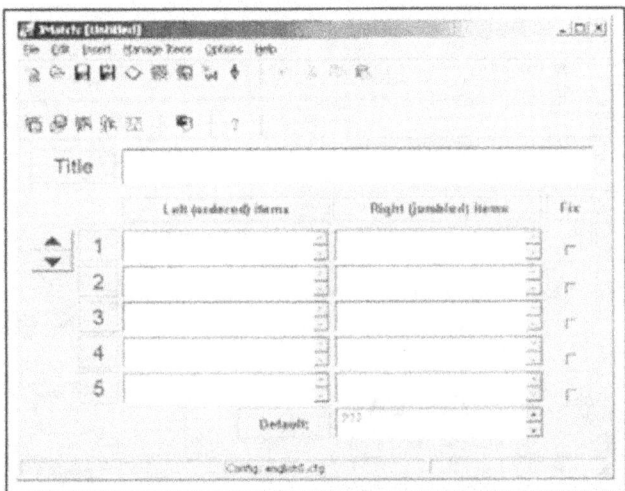

Using JCloze

1. Click on JCloze. The screen will appear formatted for a fill-in-the-blank exercise.

Figure 4.44: JCloze

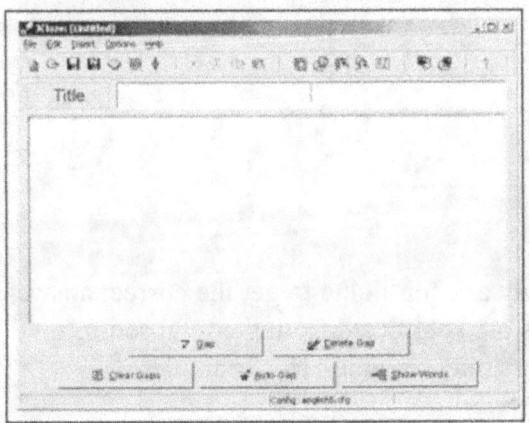

2. Key in title of the test.
3. Key in the text that you wish for the students to read. This may be a paragraph, or it may be individual questions.
4. Highlight the area of the text where you wish to create a gap.
5. Click on Gap. (You will know where you have added a gap because the word(s) will be highlighted in red and underlined.)

Chapter 4: Assessment Tools to Improve Classroom Instruction 79

Figure Figure 4.45: Creating a Gap

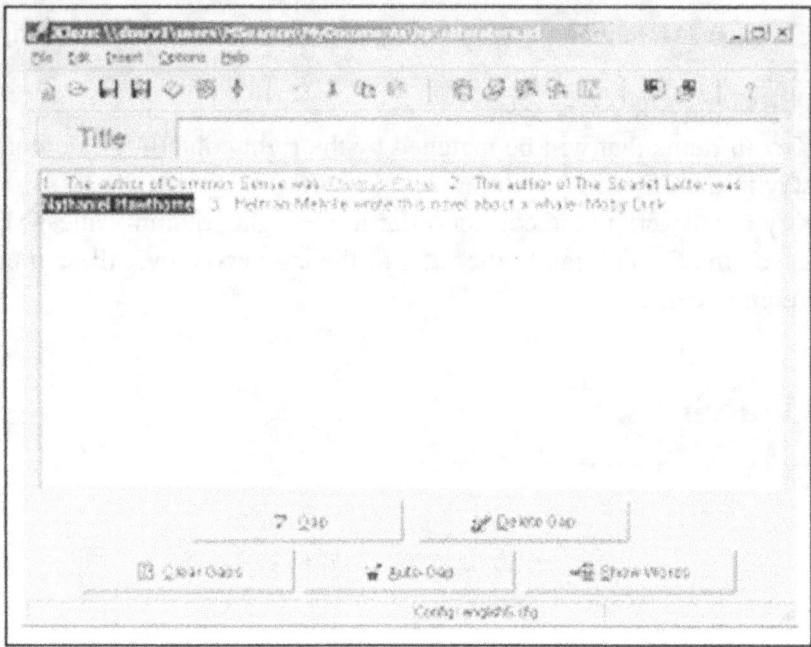

6. When you click on Gap, the following screen will pop up:

Figure 4.46: Gapped Words Alternative

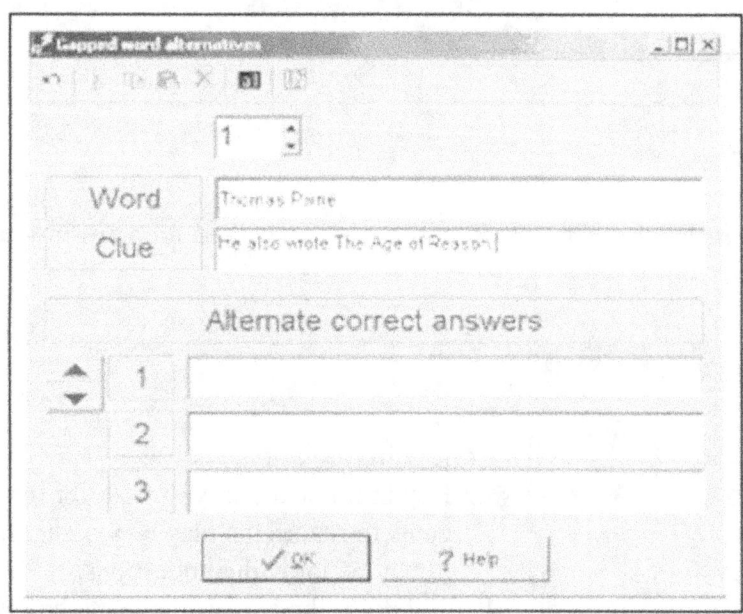

7. Add a clue. Students may ask for a clue to get the correct answer. (If a clue is requested, points are subtracted from the total score.)
8. Alternate correct answers may be added (for example, you might add Paine or T. Paine).

Chapter 5

Worksheet Wonders and More

> *"It's not the hours you put in your work that counts, it's the work you put in the hours."*
> —*Sam Ewing*

As we strive to challenge each student to achieve greater academic success than ever before, timesavers become more important. Technology is a great tool to use as we reinforce learning. In Chapter 4, we discussed using assessments to reinforce skills and facts that are learned. In this chapter, we move to worksheets—the much-maligned technique that has been criticized repeatedly as drill-and-kill.

What Do Students Know?

Getting students to engage in learning is encouraging them to reveal what they don't know. The core of professional responsibility is to evaluate what students have learned and to respond to that learning.

Why Use Worksheets?

Relying on worksheets for initial learning is poor teaching. We are sure you would agree that engaging students in active, inquiry-based, discovery learning is a far superior instructional strategy. But, let's not dismiss worksheets so readily. Do they have a purpose? Indeed, they do. Worksheets are an excellent way of reinforcing learning. Worksheets are also good tools for scaffolding the learning as students move to thoughtful interaction with the content. Often they are used to model the thinking process and to make it more visible.

Good teachers never use worksheets to pass the time. If we use worksheets to enrich classroom practices, we must be certain that we have used instructional strategies that "hook" students. Actively engaging a student in a curriculum of depth, not breadth, piques curiosity: *How can this be so? Why?* A worksheet, no matter how well designed, cannot do that. The use of worksheets must be done in moderation.

When Is the Use of a Worksheet Appropriate?

Worksheets should be viewed as an appropriate instructional strategy in the delivery of all curricula. Through a thoughtful and systemic use of worksheets, teachers positively affect student achievement by:

1. Supporting instruction based on learning objectives and facts.
2. Ensuring that all students experience success at some level. Our increasing heterogeneous classes require that we have a good mix of skill reinforcement as well as activities that allow us to analyze that information in meaningful ways and to manipulate it in a new way.
3. Providing tools which address the skill gaps that the student may have in the curriculum (if I don't know multiplication, can I learn division?).

Teachers need to use worksheets within the context with which they are most comfortable. As a teacher spirals the subject area content with depth and higher sophistication, worksheets are an appropriate means to reinforce the basic facts that a student must understand in order to comprehend the larger picture. It is a harsh reality. Some facts need to be learned—through memorization techniques or through repetition.

Good teachers have mastered the mixing of basic facts with the "big picture." Some teachers use worksheets for homework—reinforcing the new material that has been presented in class. Other teachers use them as bridge activities. What needs to be reviewed before moving into a new activity? Whether the initial forays into worksheet use are in reinforcement or in review, technology makes the use of the worksheet easier than ever before.

Enhancing Instruction

As teachers continue to work on grade level academic standards with students, worksheets can enhance instruction by saving the teacher time. Using the worksheet generator, students can create their own quizzes and exercises to challenge their peers. Let the students create worksheets to review material. Set up a Knowledge Bowl—two collaborative teams ask each other questions from generated worksheets that they have created. The team with the most answers wins.

Quick and easy worksheets, appropriate to the grade level, may be found in abundance on the Web. There are literally thousands of sites. Teachers can expend a great deal of energy and large amounts of time just exploring them.

Some sites are subscription based. Pay a fee and you are granted access to a large collection of pre-developed worksheets. Other sites are free. It is these *free* sites that we will focus on in this chapter. Teachers spend too much money of their own as it is on instructional materials for their classrooms. The ability to access worksheets is not something that needs to be paid for by the teacher.

A review of sites that specialize in generating worksheets leads us to sites that are subject specific (math, for example has hundreds of sites) or grade specific (elementary sites abound). Limiting our search to those sites that can be used for multiple subject areas and grade levels, three sites stand above the rest.

Worksheet Generator

One of our favorite worksheet sites is located at the Teacher Tool section of Discovery.com <http://school.discovery.com/teachingtools/worksheetgenerator/index.html>. At Discovery School's Worksheet Generator site, a teacher can create a custom worksheet for almost any subject and grade level. Additionally, the teacher can adapt one of the ready-made worksheets. The features that make this site stand out are many. With the many custom vocabulary lists, the table of elements for example, a teacher can copy and paste the list into multiple worksheet formats. The site allows you to register (free) and save your worksheets at the site, print out the worksheet without saving it for future use, or download your worksheets to your own computer.

Figure 5.1: Worksheet Generator

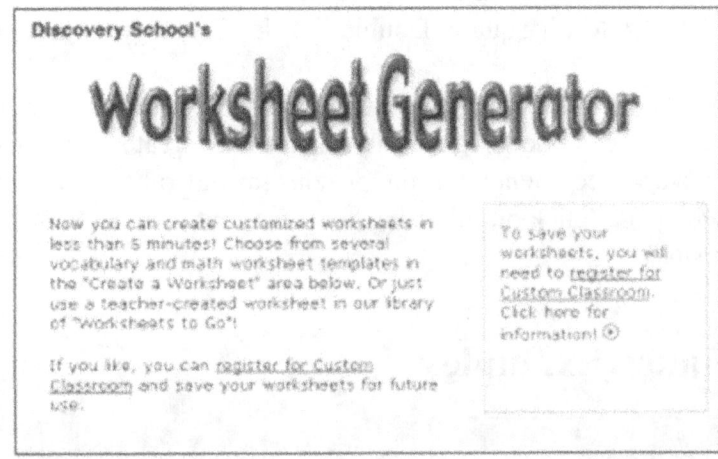

The lists of worksheets include blanks, fill-in-the-blank, matching, mix up, multiple choice, scramble, and word chop. In math, the selection includes addition, subtraction, multiplication and F O I L (First Outside Inside Last—a method of solving equations). The directions for creating each of these worksheets are clear. In addition, there are samples of each worksheet type.

The teacher user may also create different versions of the same worksheet by creating one worksheet and then clicking the back button on the browser and clicking the Create button again. That action scrambles the data that has been originally entered into the worksheet. If, for example, a teacher is using the data from the Table of Elements (a large number of terms) and is creating a 10–15 word worksheet, the click Back, click Create sequence will use additional terms in creating the new worksheet.

The ready-made worksheets are in nine categories: Art, Business/Careers, English, Health, Languages, Math, Science, Social Studies, and Technology. The worksheets span various grade levels—from a Parts of Speech worksheet to a *Romeo and Juliet* matching exercise.

Figure 5.2: Ready-To-Go Worksheets

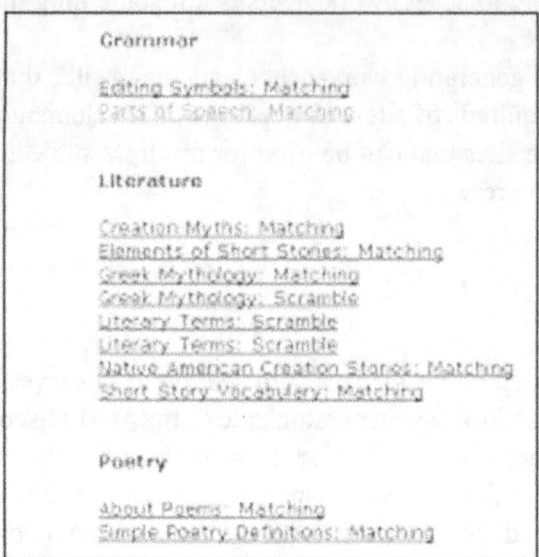

PuzzleMaker

Also located at Discovery's School Web site is PuzzleMaker <http://www.puzzlemaker.com/>. With PuzzleMaker, a teacher can create 11 difference types of puzzles. They include Mazed Things, Computer Generated Mazes, Word Search, Word Search with Hidden Message, Criss-Cross Puzzle, Number Blocks, Math Square, Double Puzzle, Cryptogram, Letter Tiles, or Fallen Phrase.

As is the case with Worksheet Generator, the directions are clear. Multiple examples and word lists for many subjects are included. Again, the teacher may create, print, and save the puzzle at the site. As with Worksheet Generator, the puzzles may also be saved in a word processing program or as a Web page (click on File, click Save As, and then name the file with a .HTM or .HTML extension).

Figure 5.3: PuzzleMaker Examples

Web Tools for Educators

Another neat site is Web Tools for Educators <http://www.teach-nology.com/web_tools/>. At this site, teachers can create crossword puzzles, word searches, word scrambles, and science labs. The one advantage of Web Tools is that a teacher may have complete control over creating a crossword puzzle. The teacher defines exactly how large the crossword should be. Secondly, the teacher enters the words in a prepared grid. The teacher can then add clues to the crossword puzzle. In order to save the file, the teacher would need to save it by clicking on File, and then clicking on Save As. There are no options for saving at the site itself.

Figure 5.4: Entering Words in a Grid

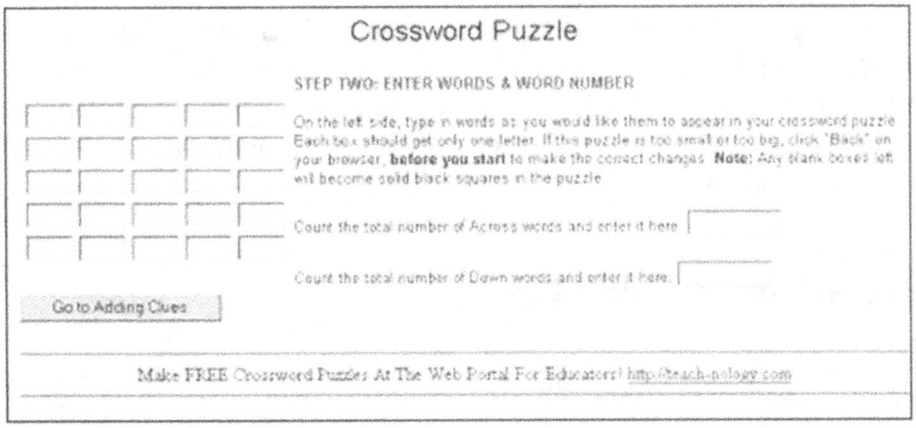

Bingo Maker

Another option at the same site <http://www.teach-nology.com/web_tools/> is the Bingo Maker. This generator allows teachers to make their own bingo cards and to generate different cards (30+ is no problem) quickly and easily. Useful in reviewing many facts (even the Table of Elements), Bingo is something that makes review of basic material kid-friendly.

Figure 5.5: Bingo Maker Generator

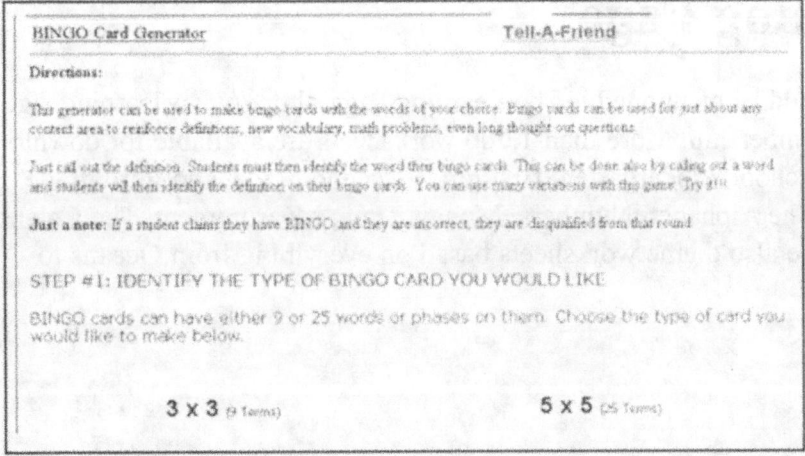

The teacher types in the words (no word lists to copy or paste are available), or even math equations, that make up the bingo game. The cards may then be printed. To print additional cards, the teacher clicks Shuffle the Words and prints each succeeding card.

Personal Educational Press

Personal Educational Press <http://www.educationalpress.org/educationalpress/Index.asp> includes no pizzazz or bells and whistles, but the site does have a clean interface and one of the best options for worksheet building. Topics available include Reading, Writing, Math, Geography, Science, U.S. Government, Spanish, and French. Teachers can create free flash cards, game boards, and quizzes. Similar to the PuzzleMaker and Worksheet Generator sites, word lists are available to be copied and pasted into a worksheet. Each general topic has its own word lists. The word lists are more extensive than those available at Worksheet Generator or PuzzleMaker.

A nice feature is that the teacher, to further customize the worksheets, can edit the word lists. Many of the word lists have corresponding answers. The table of elements, for example, has atomic symbols, atomic weights, or atomic numbers as possible answers.

The teacher may also select what will appear on the back of the flash card. One of the vocabulary lists is Greek and Latin Word Roots. The teacher may select English Meanings to be printed on the back (flash card) or may choose not to have anything printed on the back (bingo cards, for example). The teacher may also use the word lists to create a quiz, word list, bingo card, word scramble, or other item.

Figure 5.6: Selecting Word Lists

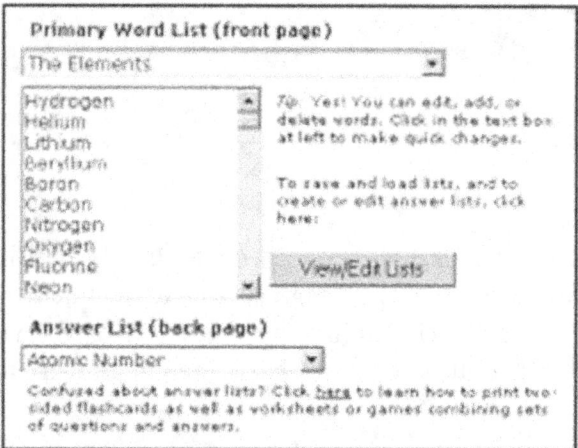

The Learning Page

Another site that should be mentioned is The Learning Page <http://www.learningpage.com>, which offers free membership. More than 1,000 worksheets are available for download. Grade levels are preschool, kindergarten, first grade, second grade, and third grade. Basic worksheets include The Alphabet, Numbers, Money, Time, Measurement, The Calendar, and The Senses. There are also theme worksheets based on everything from Oceans to Dinosaurs.

SuperKids Math Worksheet Generator

The SuperKids Math Worksheet Generator <http://www.superkids.com/aweb/tools/math/> site provides opportunities to create worksheets printed for use with addition, subtraction, mixed addition and subtraction, multiplication, division, fractions, greater than/less than, and rounding. The teacher may enter maximum and minimum values, number of digits (for subtraction, for example), number of problems for each worksheet, and then print the worksheet.

A+ Math

Another great site is A+ Math <http://www.aplusmath.com>. Math flash cards can be printed instantly through a recipe approach. The site also allows readers to customize the flash cards. Worksheets are available for addition, subtraction, multiplying fractions, geometric shapes, basic algebra, inequalities and algebra, and many other math topics. Students may generate their own worksheets, take them online, and have them corrected.

Exhibit Center

Elements of the Periodic Table: Word Scramble

Name: _____

Unscramble the following words:

1) muinumla
   _____

2) aogrn
   _____

3) racsien
   _____

4) briaum
   _____

5) rembyliul
   _____

6) ronbo
   _____

7) eronmib
   _____

8) cucamli
   _____

9) nobcra
   _____

10) uicesm
    _____

Visit Worksheet Generator at DiscoverySchool.com

If you use copy and paste and plan to save the worksheet on the Web, you must include a link to Worksheet Generator and include the Discovery School logo.

Elements of the Periodic Table: Matching Quiz

Name: _____

Match the words in the first column to the best available answer in the second column.

_____	Hydrogen	1)	He
_____	Helium	2)	Ca
_____	Lithium	3)	Al
_____	Beryllium	4)	Be
_____	Boron	5)	Na
_____	Carbon	6)	S
_____	Nitrogen	7)	F
_____	Oxygen	8)	C
_____	Fluorine	9)	Ar
_____	Neon	10)	Cl
_____	Sodium	11)	P
_____	Magnesium	12)	Ne
_____	Aluminum	13)	Li
_____	Silicon	14)	B
_____	Phosphorus	15)	Mg
_____	Sulphur	16)	H
_____	Chlorine	17)	O
_____	Argon	18)	K
_____	Potassium	19)	N
_____	Calcium	20)	Si

Visit Worksheet Generator at DiscoverySchool.com

DiscoverySchool.com

Figure 5.7: Sample Quiz from Personal Educational Press

The Elements quiz: Fill in the correct Atomic Number	Name: _____ Date: _____

Hydrogen ____

Helium ____

Lithium ____

Beryllium ____

Boron ____

Carbon ____

Nitrogen ____

Oxygen ____

Figure 5.8: Sample Flash Cards (Front) from Personal Educational Press

accretion	albedo
albedo feature	antipodal point
aphelion	arcuate
asteroid	asteroid number

Figure 5.9: Sample Flash Cards (Back) from Personal Educational Press

The ratio of the amount of light reflected by an object and the amount of incident light; a measure of the reflectivity or intrinsic brightness of an object (a white, perfectly reflecting surface would have an albedo of 1.0; a black perfectly absorbing surface would have an albedo of 0.0).	accumulation of dust and gas into larger bodies, such as stars, planets, and moons
The point that is directly on the opposite side of the planet.	A dark or light marking on the surface of an object that may not be a geological or topographical feature.
having the form of a bow; curved; arc-shaped	The point in its orbit where a planet is farthest from the Sun; when referring to objects orbiting the Earth the term apogee is used; the term apoapsis is used for orbits around other bodies. (opposite of perihelion)
Asteroids are assigned a serial number when they are discovered. It has no particular meaning except that asteroid N+1 was discovered after asteroid N.	(also "planetoid") a medium-sized rocky object orbiting the Sun; smaller than a planet, larger than a meteoroid

Figure 5.10: Sample Bingo Board from Personal Educational Press

conjunction	accretion	corona
albedo feature	corona	aphelion
doppler effect	catena	brown dwarf

Chapter 5: Worksheet Wonders and More

Show Me How It's Done

Using Worksheet Generator

To begin using Worksheet Generator, navigate to <http://school.discovery.com/teachingtools/worksheetgenerator/index.html>. Explore the site. Take advantage of the samples that are created for each type. As you click on view sample under Create A Worksheet, you will find that some worksheet types are better than others. For example, Mix Up can be used for sequencing events.

Figure 5.11: Discovery School's Worksheet Generator

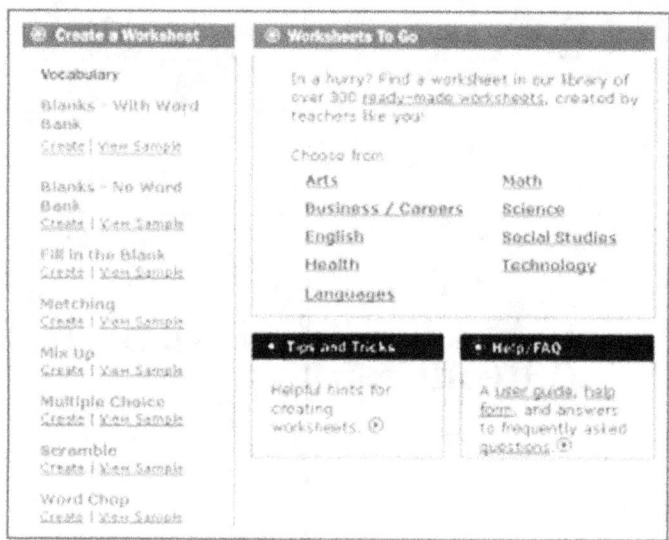

1. Determine whether you wish to create your own worksheet or whether you wish to use one that has been created by another teacher.
2. To select one created previously, click on the subject area under Worksheets To Go.
3. To create your own worksheet, click on the type of worksheet (Blanks, Fill-in-the-Blank, Addition, etc.) under Create a Worksheet.
4. The directions for creating the worksheet are very specific. Try it out!

Figure 5.12: Create a Worksheet

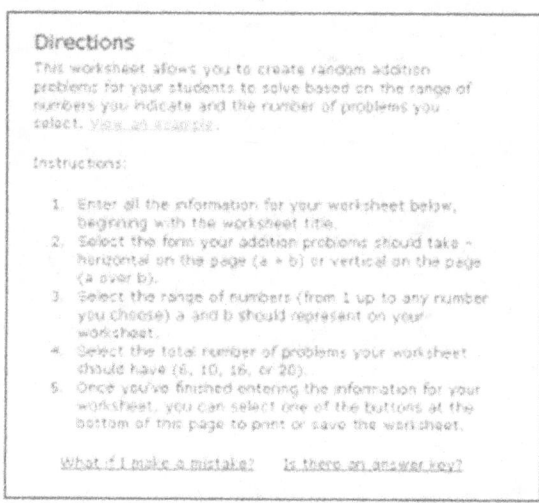

5. After you have created your worksheet, you will be given two options, Create a Printable Version and Preview and Save to My Account.

94 Technology Timesavers: Simple Steps to Increasing Classroom Productivity

Figure 5.13: Print Your Worksheet

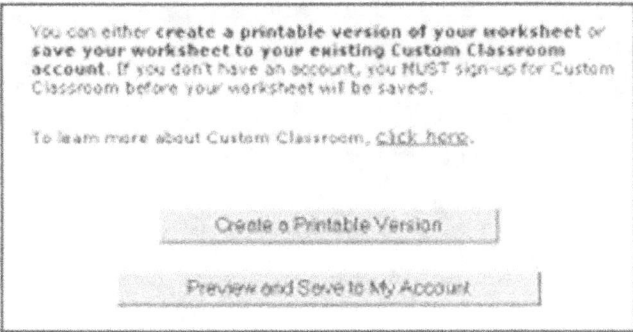

6. If you click Create a Printable Version, you will see a preview of the worksheet that you have created.

Saving Your Worksheet

7. Saving your worksheet may be accomplished in one of four ways. First, you may save it to the Custom Classroom account that you have created. The link for creating a Custom Classroom account can be found at the top right of Discovery School's Worksheet Generator, PuzzleMaker, Quiz Center, or Lesson Plan page. The same account works for all of them.
8. Second, if you wish to save the printable version to your own computer, you may copy and paste it to a word processing program and save it—click Edit on the menu bard, click Select All, click Edit again, and then click Copy. Open your word processing program—click Edit, click Paste. The worksheet may now be saved to your computer files as you would any other document.
9. Third, you may also save it by clicking the File, Save As menu. However, you would have to save it as a text file (.txt), which will cause the document to lose its formatting.
10. Fourth, you may save it as an .HTM or .HTML file and post it on your Web site. In order to post the worksheet on your site, however, Discovery School's Worksheet Generator requires that you provide a link back to the Discovery School site and that you include a logo. To comply with these conditions, click the File, Save As menu. When the Save Web Page box comes up, use the Save In drop down box to select where you wish to save the document. Then click Save As Type in the drop down box, and select Web Page Complete. The link and the Discovery School logo will be saved along with the .HTM document.

Figure 5.14: Options for Saving Your Worksheet

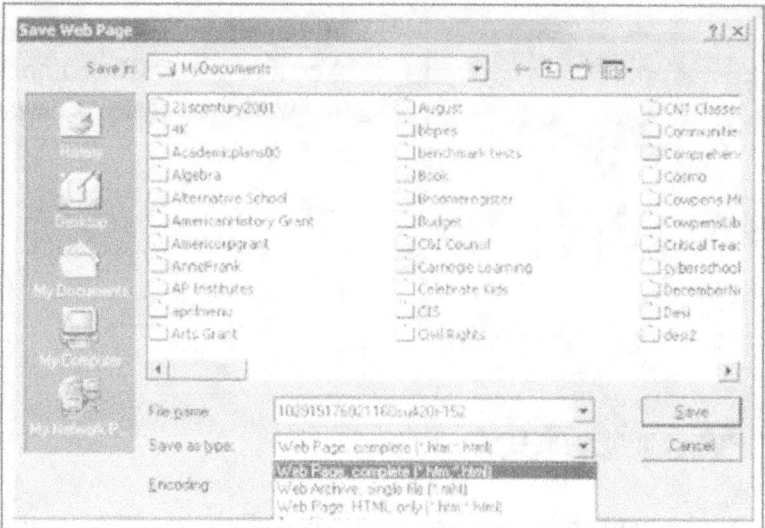

Creating a Worksheet Using PuzzleMaker Vocabulary Lists

Another quick and easy option for creating worksheets is to use a PuzzleMaker vocabulary list <http://school.discovery.com/puzzlemaker/wordlists/>. There are four categories of lists: History, Holidays, Science, and Discovery Channel School Lesson Plans Vocabulary words. This example demonstrates how to create a matching quiz.

1. Click on the vocabulary list category.
2. Click on the vocabulary list and copy and paste it into the worksheet format that you wish to use. If you wish to put answers in the worksheet, separate the words with commas.
3. Worksheet Generator formats the quiz for you. Click Create a Printable Version or Preview and Save to My Account.

Figure 5.15: Create a Matching Quiz Using Word Lists

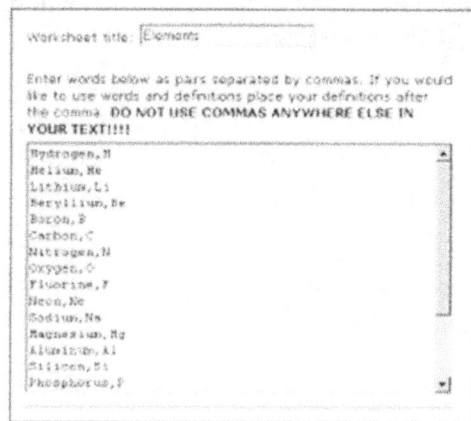

96 *Technology Timesavers: Simple Steps to Increasing Classroom Productivity*

One Click Does It

PuzzleMaker generates mazes and number blocks automatically.

1. To access the wonderful mazes available, click on the link to Cool Mazes on the home page of <www.puzzlemaker.com>.

Figure 5.16: Cool Mazes

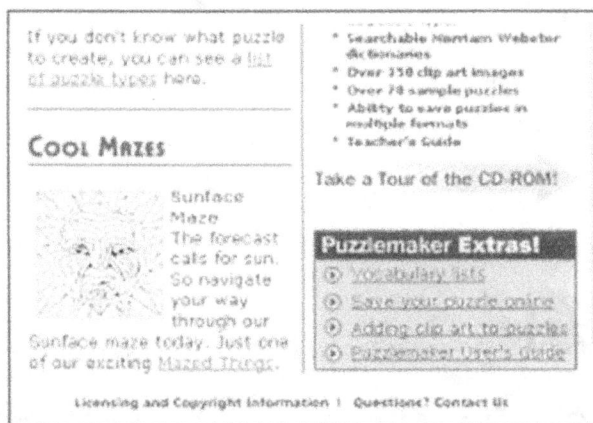

2. A teacher may print up to 50 copies of the Mazed things. If more than 50 copies will be distributed, permission is required.
3. The mazes are in three general categories: animals, holidays, and miscellaneous.

Figure 5.17: Animal Maze Collection

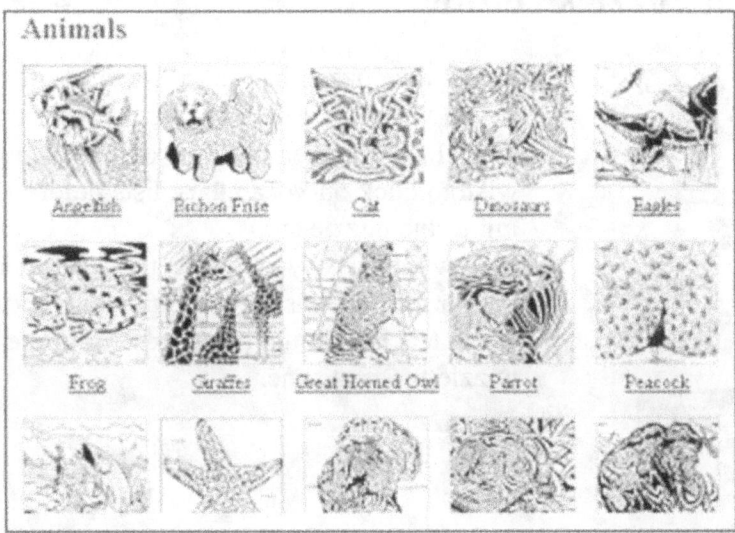

Creating Other Mazes

4. If you wish to create an original maze, click on Mazes in the drop down box on the home page.
5. The PuzzleMaker Advanced Maze Creation screen opens.
6. A step-by-step tutorial takes you through the creation of your maze.

Chapter 5: Worksheet Wonders and More 97

Figure 5.18: Advanced Maze Creation

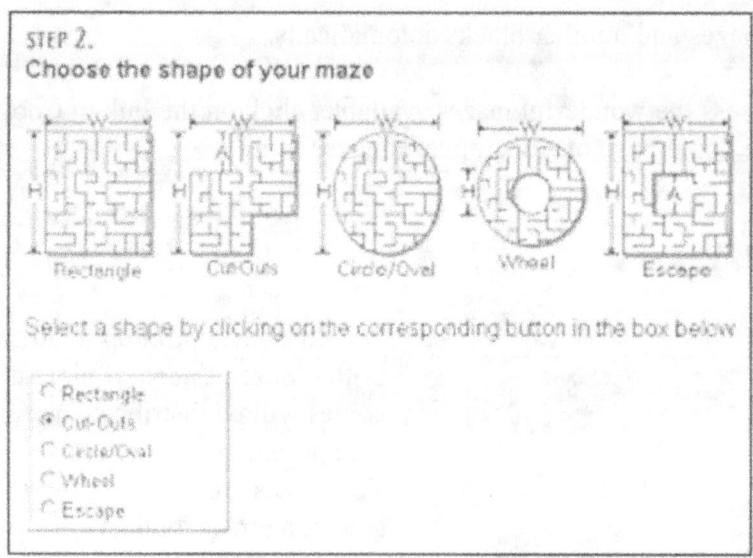

Creating Other Puzzles

7. To access other puzzles, click on the drop down menu under Create Puzzles Online.

Figure 5.19: Create Puzzles Online

8. Select the puzzle that you wish to create.
9. If you wish to create a puzzle that uses a vocabulary list (word search, for example), you may wish to click on Vocabulary lists before navigating to the puzzle site.
10. Follow the step-by-step directions for creating the puzzle. The instructions are clear enough that a teacher should be successful in creating a puzzle the first time.

Copying or Printing Your Puzzle

11. As you complete the steps, you will be asked for the type of output (how do you want to copy the puzzle) that you would like for your puzzle.
12. There are three options: HTML, text, and lowercase text.
13. If you wish to use the puzzle online, click the HTML choice.

Figure 5.20: Selecting the Output Style

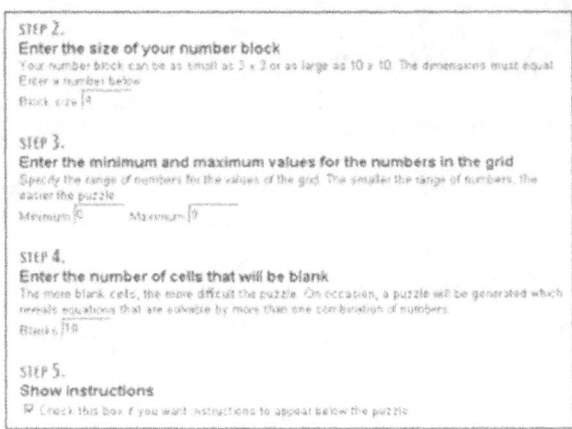

Personal Educational Press

<http://www.educationalpress.org/educationalpress/Index.asp>

At Personal Educational Press, the instructions are also easy for a beginner to use.

1. Before a user selects a particular format (bingo cards, study sheets, word scramble, word search, etc.) to use, he or she is asked to select a vocabulary list.
2. The teacher may select from numerous word lists in reading, writing, math, geography, science, and government.
3. After the selection is made, the teacher may select a corresponding list to include on the back of the card or on a study sheet. In the figure below, the teacher may ask that the definition of each word be printed on the back of each card.

Figure 5.21: Vocabulary Lists and Answer Lists

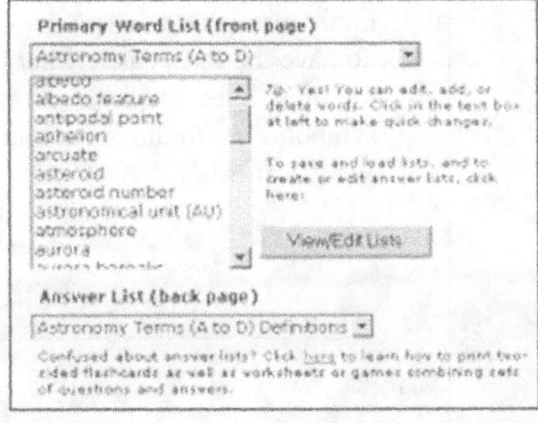

4. The teacher may add or subtract word lists by clicking on the View/Edit Lists button.
5. After the vocabulary list is ready, click on the type of review sheet that you would like.
6. If you click Study Sheet, the vocabulary list that you selected on the first page will automatically be used.
7. Several selections of how the study sheet should appear are available.
8. To print a study sheet that includes the terms and the definitions, click the Number word/Answer pairs selection at the top left of the page.

Chapter 5: Worksheet Wonders and More 99

Figure 5.22: Study Sheet Options

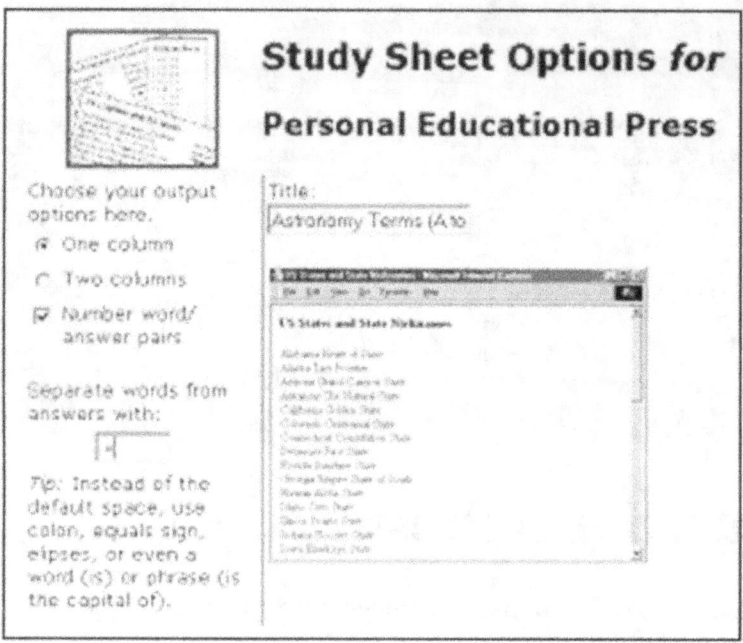

Creating Flash Cards

Flash cards and bingo boards may be easily created as well.

1. After selecting a vocabulary list, select Flash cards.
2. If you wish to make double-sided flash cards, select Double-Sided flash cards in the options box.

Figure 5.23: Flash Card Selection

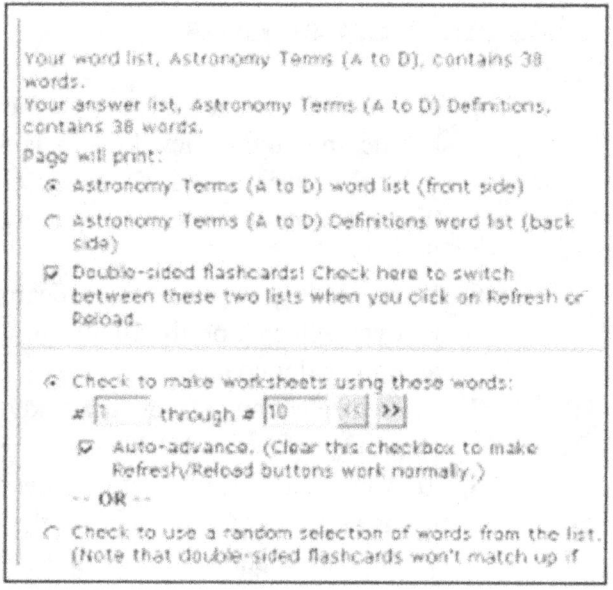

3. If your word list is long, you may wish to print the cards several times in order to include all of the words.
4. To have the flash card maker print multiple times, click the refresh symbol or go to the menu and click View, Refresh.

Chapter 6

Making the Grade

> *"Only the mediocre are always at their best."*
>
> —*Jean Giraudoux*

Why Assess?

What is the purpose of classroom assessment? Most of us would probably agree that the purpose of assessment is to find out what students know and are able to do. After some reflection we would probably add that assessment provides us a way to improve instruction and to measure student achievement. Ideally, we assess in order to measure how much the student has learned. Effective teachers use assessment information to revise instruction based on student performance. A well-constructed evaluation allows us to examine the results and to identify instructional practices that must be changed to increase student achievement.

Good assessments guide teachers as they plan the next step in learning. Often developmental tools, assessments alert students to key concepts that they must learn. The difficulties with assessment, however, are two fold. First, the emphasis is often placed the issuance of grades. Second, not everything that is taught can be assessed easily. A case in point is the assessment of Web-based learning.

Grades Are Important

Grades are important. We like to say that they are not and that what is important is what the students learn. Do we really believe that? How is assessment used? If assessments are used as guideposts that point the direction to what is taught, then student learning is truly emphasized. Generating specific criteria of what needs to be learned and then developing the perfect assessment of what was learned require time and a good understanding of the specific skills that contribute to the learning standards.

Grades are important—to students and to parents. When we assess students, we need to acknowledge that. Whenever any assignment is made, students will clamor for specifics:

"So, what's going to be on the test?"
"Will this count?"
"That's not fair! I deserved an "A." I worked hard on that paper."

Sometimes it seems that all students focus on are the grades as the measure of what has been learned. We have to ask ourselves, do our assessments really measure student learning? Do we focus on what is important for the child to know and be able to do? Or do we emphasize the part of the learning that is most quickly assessed? *("Grades are due tomorrow at noon—don't be late.")*

Teaching to the Test

Grading collaborative learning projects and essays stymie us at times. We do not seem to do a good job of telling students what we expect them to learn. If we clarify our goals for students and provide effective and frequent feedback about how to improve, student achievement will increase. Is it teaching to the test? While we would agree that there is more to school than just getting the right answer, we would also have to say that a well-designed assessment does point to what the child has learned.

If a teacher aligns testing and evaluating with the academic standards that must be learned, student achievement will increase. Assessments are tools that define what has been taught and what has been learned. In the best scenario, assessments are also developmental tools that define future instruction and future learning.

Using Rubrics to Define Instruction

We would all agree that we need to do a better job of telling students what they are expected to learn. We gain wisdom by learning from our past mistakes and from our successes.

A teacher may struggle to explain concisely and concretely why an essay or a project was "given" an "A" or a "B." Why is it so difficult to explain when it seems so evident? Why can't we explain the difference to a student or to a student's parent? It may be that we did not carefully define what our expectations were for student learning before the assignment was undertaken. It may be that we have a clear picture of the overall outcome but cannot define the specific skills that contribute to that overall picture.

Increasingly, as states have focused on academic standards, the rubric (a description of levels of student performance) has become more and more popular. Although difficult to construct, the rubric is a wonderful tool. The difficulty in creating a rubric is breaking down the big picture into its component parts, the skills that must be demonstrated by the student for successful completion of the project or the essay. For the student, a rubric is a training model. The criteria establish what the student must accomplish to receive a specific grade.

Once the criteria for the work have been established, the well-designed rubric makes success more achievable. The teacher should not be the only one to determine what a student has learned. That determination should be a process that includes all of the stakeholders in the classroom. Rubrics lend themselves nicely to self and peer evaluation.

By providing an established uniform set of criteria in the rubric, the teacher communicates information to students about what is expected on the project and how to go about meeting the challenge. In very simple terms, *if you know how to get a grade, you know what is expected.*

Rubrics, then, should be given to students before they begin the work.

Three Tools to Develop Rubrics

Three of the most accommodating rubric generators to use are RubiStar, ClassWeb, and Rubric Maker.

	RubiStar	**ClassWeb**	**Rubric Maker**
Easy to use	Yes	No	Yes
Teacher friendly	Yes	Yes	Yes
Provides examples of commonly used rubrics	Yes	Yes	No—provides one example
Rubric may be saved on Web server	Yes	Yes	No
Rubric may be modified before it is saved	Yes	Yes	No
Aligns rubrics to state standards	No	No	No
Automatic scoring	Yes	Yes	No
Converts rubric to Web page	Yes	Yes	Yes

RubiStar

http://rubistar.4teachers.org

One of the easiest of the three rubric generators is RubiStar, a free service. The simplicity stems from its straightforward presentation. The first page clearly states the purpose, offers tutorials, provides sample rubrics, and provides information on analyzing rubric data. A teacher can hit the Web site and quickly find a rubric for almost any project. Through experience in working with teachers on Web-based learning projects, we have found that teachers are comfortable with the simplicity of the Web site. Teachers, even those who are not familiar with building rubrics, find success quickly on this Web site. As Figure 6.1 illustrates, the sample rubrics focus on a common exercise for which a teacher would most likely want to provide a rubric to students—for example, collaborative projects, multimedia projects, and The Six Traits of Writing model.

Figure 6.1: Sample Topics on RubiStar

SCIENCE	RESEARCH & WRITING	WORK SKILLS
Lab Report	Story Writing	Collaborative Work Skills
Science Fair	Letter Writing	
Building A Bridge	Group Planning - Research Project	
	Research Report	
	6 + 1 Writing Model	
MATH	ART	MUSIC

A key advantage of RubiStar is that the users may easily modify rubrics for their own uses. The teacher then has three options for using the rubric: (1) saving to the RubiStar Web server, (2) downloading it to save on another Web server, or (3) printing out the rubric without saving.

Other key features are that rubrics are available in Spanish as well as English. Numeric and descriptive rating scales may be used and modified. Descriptive categories may be selected from a menu and modified as well. If multimedia project is selected, for example, the teacher may select from these descriptors: Content, Mechanics, Attractiveness, Mechanics, Organization, Oral Presentation, Originality, Workload, Requirements, Presentation, Sources, and Rough Draft. Sample language for each rating is inserted for each of the descriptor categories that is selected. Teachers may then modify to suit their own project requirements. A teacher may also customize the rubric by adding other descriptor categories and rows.

Created rubrics may be saved as a Web page and uploaded to the teacher's own Web site or printed for classroom use and explanation. RubiStar is an excellent method for teachers who are unaccustomed to evaluating group performance to clarify their expectations and requirements before students undertake the work.

ClassWeb

<http://www.landmark-project.com/classweb/tools/rubric_builder.php3>

ClassWeb, a free service of the Landmark Project, provides teachers the opportunity to create a rubric from scratch. A teacher must be more patient in using ClassWeb. The opening page is an information form that must be completed before continuing. For those who are new to building rubrics, the opening page can be intimidating. One of the questions asks for the number of objectives that the rubric will contain, while another question asks for the number of performance indicators in the rubric.

Figure 6.2: ClassWeb Rubric Builder

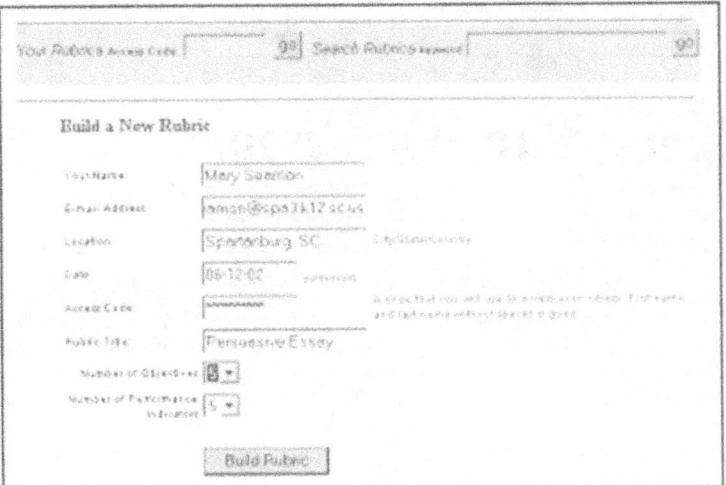

Teacher Rubric Maker

<http://teachers.teach-nology.com/web_tools/rubrics/>

The Teacher Rubric Maker is simple to use. Currently, 20+ rubrics are available. The site promises additional rubrics in the coming months. The quality of these rubrics is good. However, there is not as much flexibility in using these rubrics as there are with the previous two examples. In order to modify these rubrics, the creator must click on the Save As command. The rubric may be saved as an HTML file and may then be edited with Web editing software or saved as a text file. A copy of the rubric may also be copied and pasted into a word processing program and may then be modified.

As Figure 6.3 illustrates, the interface is teacher-friendly. The rubrics are on topics that teachers request most often.

Figure 6.3: Rubric Samples from Rubric Generator

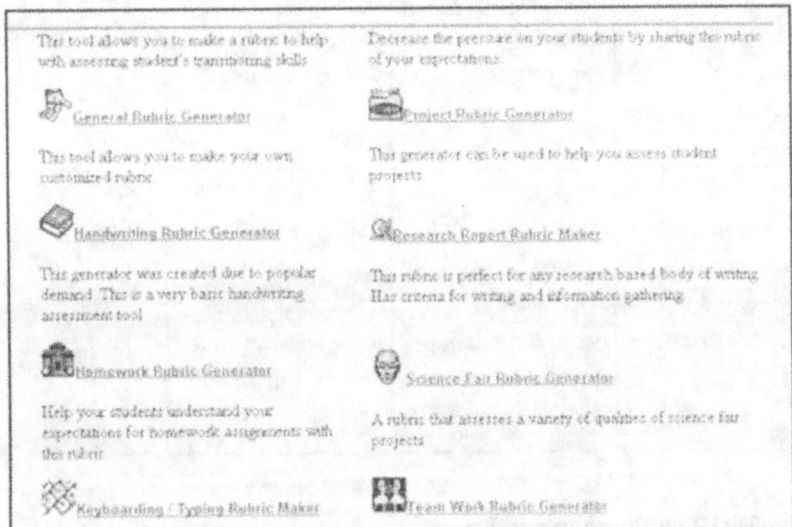

Exhibit Center

Rubric on Edgar Allan Poe Report

Student Name _____

CATEGORY	Excellent	Good	Satisfactory	Needs Improvement
Quality of Information	Information clearly relates to the main topic. It includes several supporting details and/or examples.	Information clearly relates to the main topic. It provides 1-2 supporting details and/or examples.	Information clearly relates to the main topic. No details and/or examples are given.	Information has little or nothing to do with the main topic.
Paragraph Construction	All paragraphs include introductory sentence, explanations or details, and concluding sentence.	Most paragraphs include introductory sentence, explanations or details, and concluding sentence.	Paragraphs included related information but are typically not constructed well.	Paragraphing structure was not clear and sentences are not typically related within the paragraphs.
Internet Use	Successfully uses suggested Internet links to find information and to navigate within these sites easily without assistance.	Usually able to use suggested Internet links to find information and navigates within these sites easily without assistance.	Occasionally able to use suggested Internet links to find information and navigates within these sites easily without assistance.	Needs assistance or supervision to use suggested Internet links and/or to navigate within these sites.
Organization	Information is very organized with well-constructed paragraphs and subheadings.	Information is organized with well-constructed paragraphs.	Information is organized, but paragraphs are not well constructed.	The information appears to be disorganized.
Sources	All sources (information and graphics) are accurately documented in the desired format.	All sources (information and graphics) are accurately documented, but a few are not in the desired format.	All sources (information and graphics) are accurately documented, but many are not in the desired format.	Some sources are not accurately documented.

<http://www.spa3.k12.sc.us/poeubric.htm>

WebQuest Evaluation Form

	Proficient	Competent	Basic
Frames the Essential Question	The essential question scaffolds learning, spanning Bloom's Taxonomy; the learner is encouraged to wonder; the learner is encouraged to invent his/her own solution; the essential question builds on prior knowledge.	The question spans the lower levels of Bloom's Taxonomy—knowledge, comprehension, and application; the student is able to quickly reach a conclusion in response to the question; does not attempt to have students make judgment or evaluation.	The question can be answered directly; the focus of the question is knowledge and comprehension; the question has one obvious answer (i.e., Is slavery good or bad?).
Connects WebQuest to Academic Standards at developmentally appropriate grade level	WebQuest is interdisciplinary with clearly targeted standards; standards are directly correlated to the tasks.	WebQuest is not interdisciplinary; no effort is made to connect to other disciplines; standards are related to the WebQuest.	WebQuest lists multiple items from standards that are peripherally connected to the topic; standards listed are not appropriate to the WebQuest.
Engaging Scenario & Tasks	The scenario and task are engaging for students; the task provides sufficient background information to excite the interest of students; the procedures are clearly outlined.	The scenario is interesting; the tasks are not clearly defined; inadequate background information is supplied for each role; directions are clear.	The scenario is one-dimensional; the task requires a student to research at the knowledge or comprehension level; directions are vague.
Relevant Internet sources at appropriate grade level for students	All information listed is relevant information; sources are differentiated for each role; puts meaning of the problem in personal, social, or community perspectives; sources are at an appropriate reading level for students.	Information listed includes relevant and irrelevant materials; uses a limited number of sources; sites do not encourage reflection; sites may be developmentally inappropriate.	Links to sites and materials are not directly connected to the assignment; uses one source; interprets meaning from one source; does not provide information for students to analyze or interpret.
Roles are interesting and create dissonance	The WebQuest introduces characters who would interact with the information in the "real world;" there are several characters; the characters are unique; characters have different points of view on the subject.	The characters are similar in belief or thought; there is insufficient background information; there are two or fewer roles; the character is clearly "invented" and would not be involved in the scenario in the real world.	There are no clearly defined characters; characters are stereotypical or one-dimensional; background information is the same for all characters; there is one role in the WebQuest.
Produces Product Connected to Assignment	The description of the product is clearly and coherently presented, product is clearly related to task; product is unique and would clearly stretch the group's thinking.	The product does not encourage students to reflect and evaluate contrasting points of view; product is similar to other products that have been produced.	Product is not clearly connected to the question.
Creativity	Student would be able to generate multiple approaches of looking at the problem; student would be challenge to demonstrate different approaches.	Student would be able to demonstrate one clear approach to understanding the problem; does not ask students to draw conclusion.	Student copies and pastes from the Internet without discrimination; product demonstrates little connection to the question; product does not show reflection.

<http://www.spa3.k12.sc.us/webquestrubric.htm>

Persuasive Essay Rubric

	Inadequate	Adequate	Good	Superior
Thesis	No clear thesis statement	Vague or unclear thesis	Identifiable, clear thesis	Easily identifiable, clear thesis
Research	Much or most research information is inaccurate or incomplete.	Weak research information used to support/prove thesis.	Accurate and adequate research information used to support thesis.	Accurate and thorough research information to support/prove thesis.
Content	Little, if any, development of supporting ideas.	Ideas show a weak structure and do not flow smoothly.	All ideas are clearly written; some ideas may not support/prove thesis appropriately.	All ideas are clearly written and flow logically to support/prove thesis.
Conventions	Sentence structure, grammar, and punctuation show frequent and blatant error; frequent misspelling of commonly used words.	Sentence structure, grammar, and punctuation demonstrate a basic understanding of mechanics; frequent minor errors in spelling.	Sentence structure, grammar, and punctuation demonstrate an adequate understanding of mechanics; infrequent, minor errors in spelling.	Sentence structure, grammar, and punctuation demonstrate proficiency of mechanics; minimal or no spelling errors.

<http://www.spa3.k12.sc.us/WebQuests/Basketball/PersuasiveRubric.htm>

Show Me How It's Done

Using RubiStar

The opening page for RubiStar is straightforward. Notice that the interface is clean and uncluttered. A quick tutorial is immediately available.

Figure 6.4: RubiStar

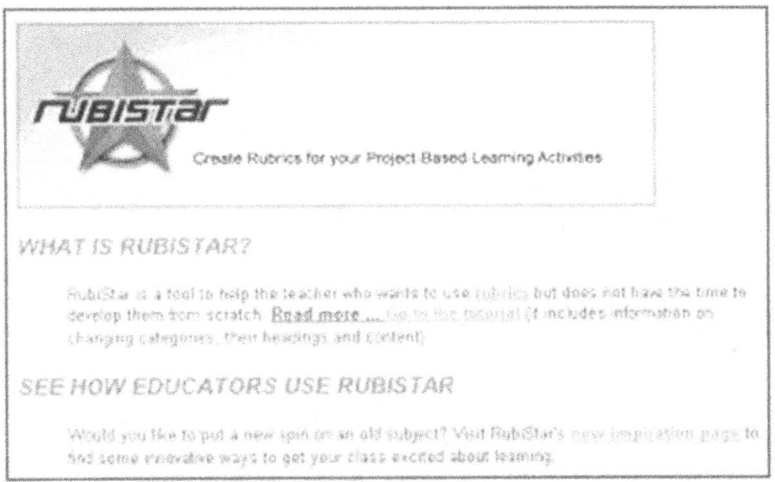

RubiStar has many sample rubrics from which the teacher may select. Clicking on a rubric will bring up another menu.

Figure 6.5: Rubric Samples

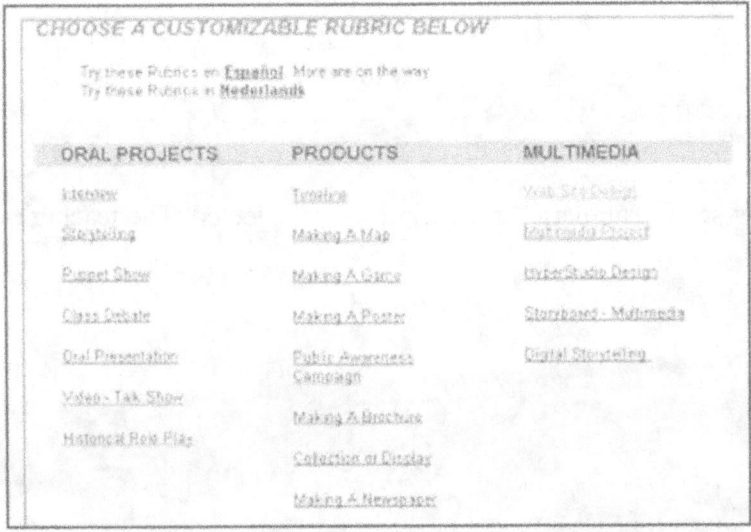

For our example, we clicked on Multimedia Project. Immediately, the rubric appears on the screen (Figure 6.5). Notice that the origin of the rubric is listed. Directions, clear and concise, follow. In teacher training sessions, we have had very little problem in introducing teachers to RubiStar. Most teachers jump in and create a rubric immediately.

Figure 6.6: Multimedia Project Rubric

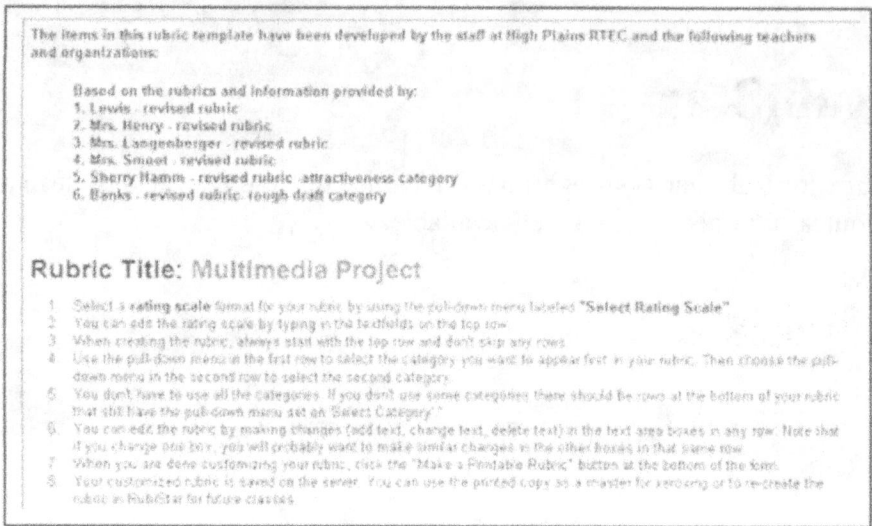

After the teacher has read the directions and has scrolled down the page, the rubric is personalized by selecting a rating scale, categories, and criteria.

Figure 6.7: Rating Scale

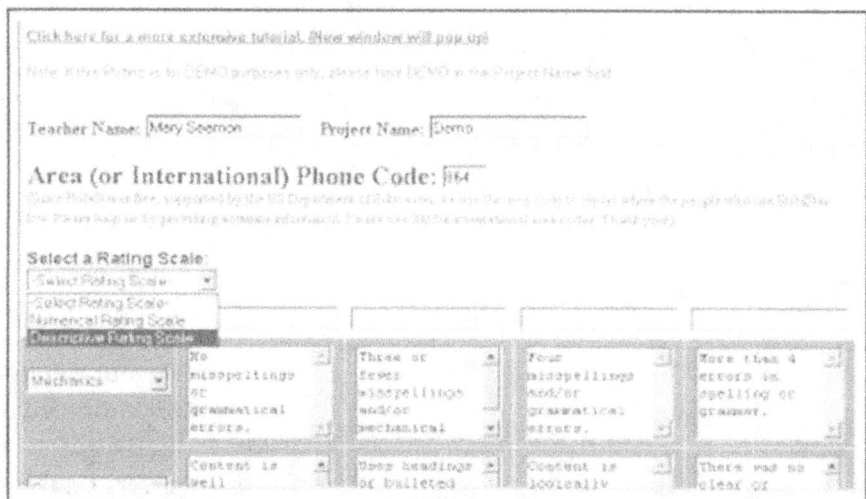

The type of rating scale—numeric or descriptive—is selected. The teacher may edit the scale after insertion.

Figure 6.8: Making Your Category Selections

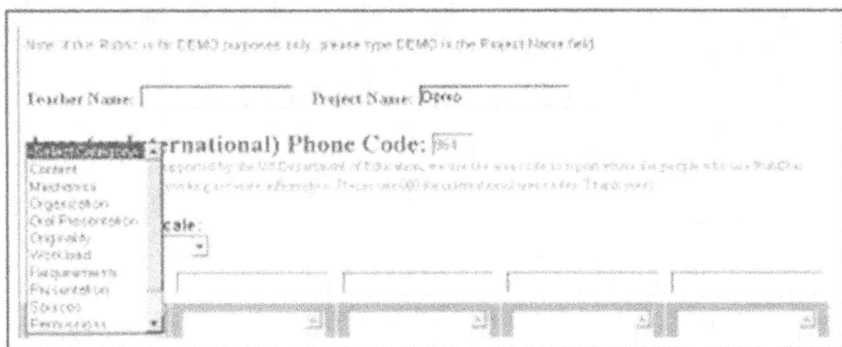

The teacher selects each of the categories to begin constructing the rubric. The teacher determines the number of categories—he or she may select as many as is appropriate for the assignment.

Figure 6.9: Rating Scale Criteria

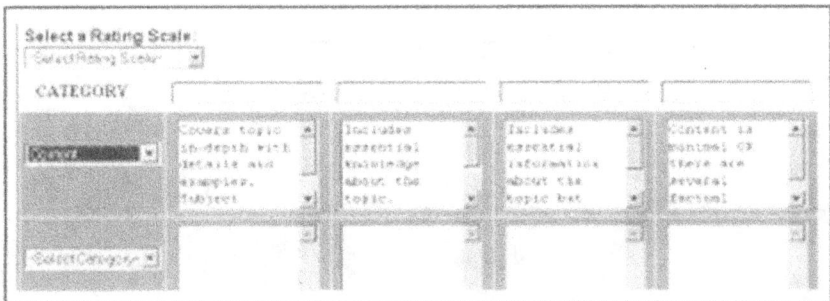

As each category is selected, sample language is inserted in each rating category. The teacher may retain the language or may edit the language as easily as if he or she was working in a word processing program.

Figure 6.10: Printing or Saving the Rubric

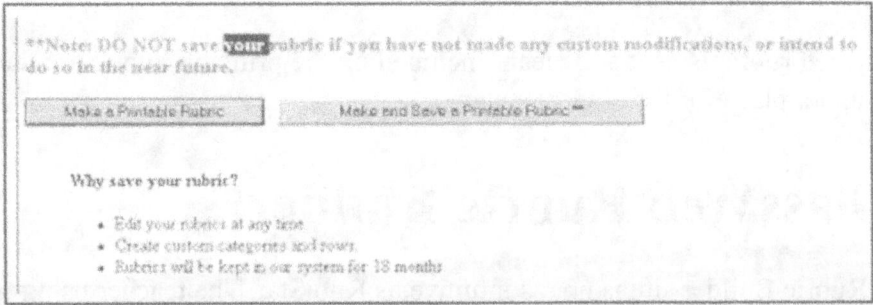

Once all the selections are made, the teacher scrolls to the end and determines whether to print the rubric or to save the rubric. The rubric may be saved at the RubiStar site or may be saved as a file to upload on the teacher's Web site. The rubric will be saved for 18 months. Rubrics that have not been customized should not be saved.

Figure 6.11: Tutorials

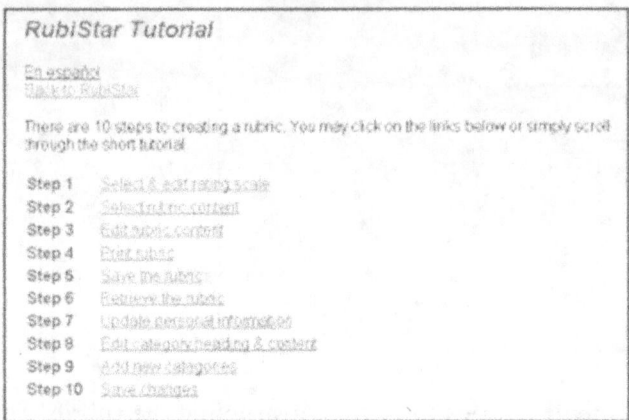

RubiStar provides extensive tutorials. However, the site is so intuitive that most teachers will find that they are able to complete the tasks with very little pre-instruction.

Figure 6.12: Completed Rubric

Multimedia Project: Demo

Teacher name: Mary Seamon

Student Name ________________

CATEGORY	Excellent	Good	Satisfactory	Needs Improvement
Mechanics	No misspellings or grammatical errors.	Three or fewer misspellings and/or mechanical errors.	Four misspellings and/or grammatical errors.	More than 4 errors in spelling or grammar.
Organization	Content is well organized using headings or bulleted lists to group related material.	Uses headings or bulleted lists to organize, but the overall organization of topics appears flawed.	Content is logically organized for the most part.	There was no clear or logical organizational structure, just lots of facts.
Presentation	Well-rehearsed with smooth	Rehearsed with fairly smooth	Delivery not smooth, but able	Delivery not smooth and

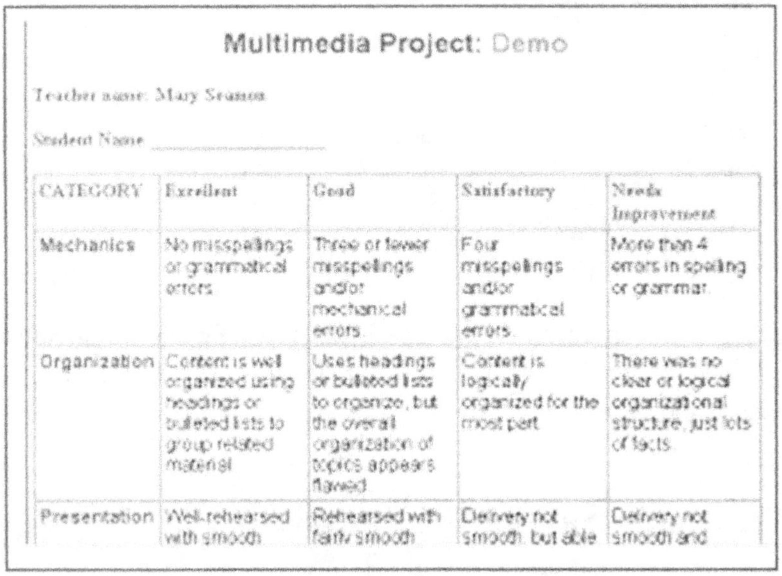

The finished rubric is neat and clean. Included on the printable rubric are the teacher's name and a place for the student's name.

Using ClassWeb Rubric Builder

The ClassWeb Rubric Builder site is not as intuitive as RubiStar. The teacher using the site has to be more familiar with the language of rubric building. The language of rubric building—performance indicator, for example—is standard, but many teachers may not be familiar with it. Using the ClassWeb Rubric Builder does produce a very nice rubric, however.

Figure 6.13: Rubric Builder Start Page

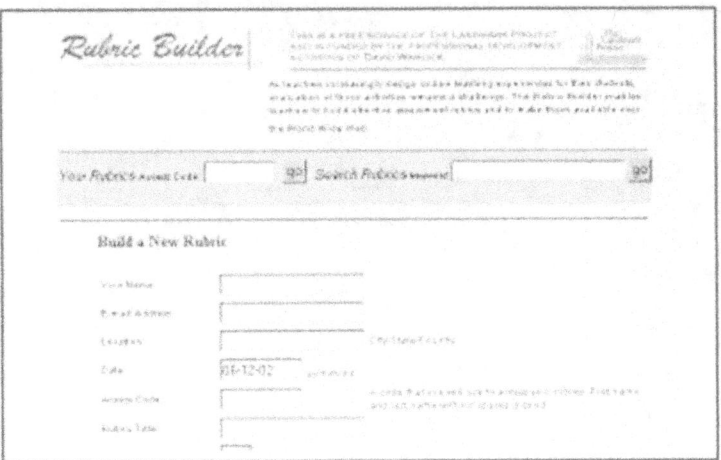

The Rubric Builder start page asks that the teacher complete an information sheet. If the site has been used previously, however, the teacher enters an access code.

The teacher may also enter key words in the Search Rubrics block to access rubrics that may have been created by other teachers. The examples cover the gamut from sophisticated to very basic. A nice feature is that a teacher may clone (adopt ownership) of a previously created rubric.

After the start page is completed with the number of objectives (what you want to assess) and performance indicators (descriptions of performance standards), the teacher clicks Build Rubric.

Performance Indicators

After Build Rubric is clicked, the next page opens with another blank form to be completed. This form contains blanks for each objective and the performance indicators. While the initial reaction of a novice rubric builder may be to gasp, there is help available. Near the top of the page, a teacher may enter keywords for the type of assessment he or she is creating and the program will search for rubrics that have been created by other teachers on the same topic. This keyword search is available on the opening Web page as well as on the second page.

Figure 6.14: Building a Rubric with ClassWeb Rubric Builder

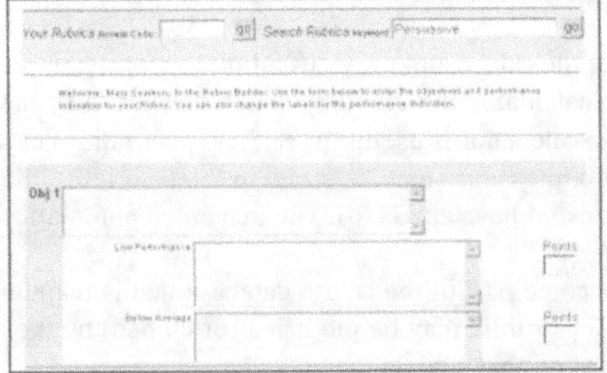

The second window opens and the teacher may enter objectives and the performance indicators to measure the objective. The teacher may also determine the number of points that each performance indicator is worth.

Chapter 6: Making the Grade 113

Figure 6.15: Completed Objectives

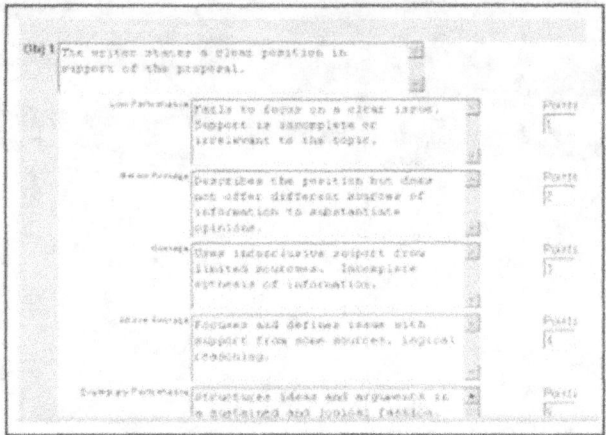

In the example in Figure 6.15, the objective is: The writer states a clear position in support of the proposal. Each level of performance (performance indicator) is entered. Point values (how much each performance indicator is worth in the evaluation) range from 1–5 in this example.

Figure 6.16: Completing Your Rubric

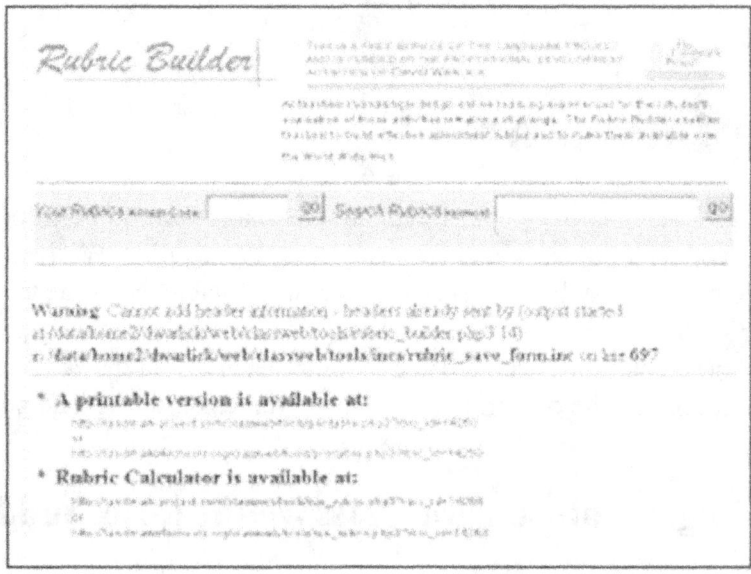

The Rubric Builder completes the rubric and provides a link to a printable version of the rubric. It also points to the rubric calculator, a method by which teachers may have the rubric automatically scored. The rubric calculator is useful for self and peer ratings especially.

After a teacher creates a rubric, the rubric may be saved to the Rubric Builder Web site, or the teacher may save the rubric and have an HTML file generated automatically for use on the teacher's own Web site.

Rubrics saved to ClassWeb become part of the rubric database that is maintained to assist other teacher to create rubrics. The rubric may be modified (or cloned) by the author or by other teachers looking for rubrics on that subject.

Figure 6.17: A Saved Rubric

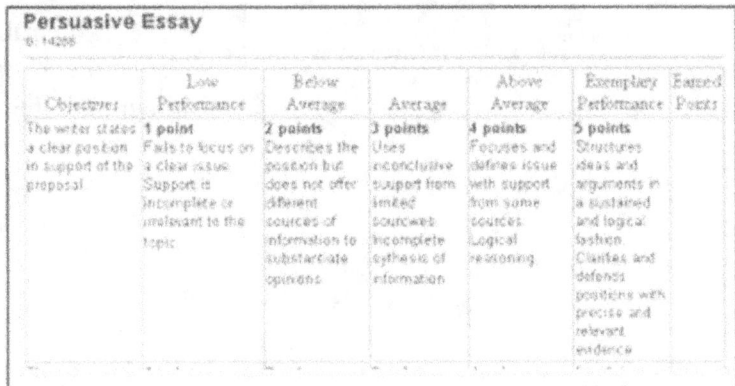

Figure 6.18: HTML Code

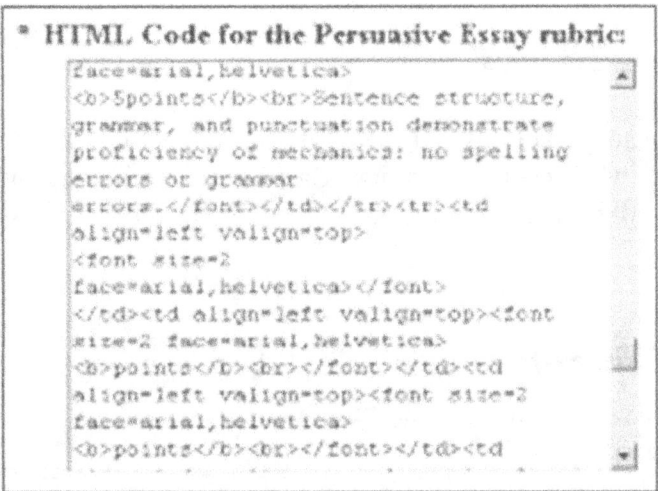

The Rubric Builder generates HTML code for the rubric, which may be used to create a Web page.

Figure 6.19: Persuasive Essay Rubric

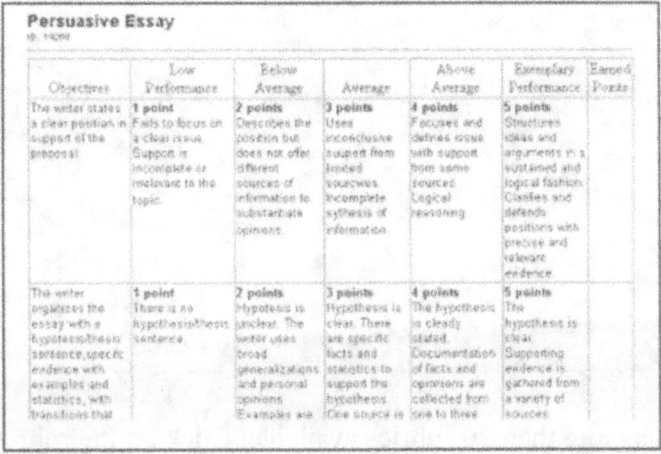

The rubric may be viewed before printing. Notice that the far right column provides a place for the evaluator—teacher, self, or peer—to indicate the number of points earned in that category. The rubric is automatically saved to the Rubric Builder site and may be accessed by the creator and others at a later time.

Chapter 6: Making the Grade 115

Figure 6.20: Calculating Score

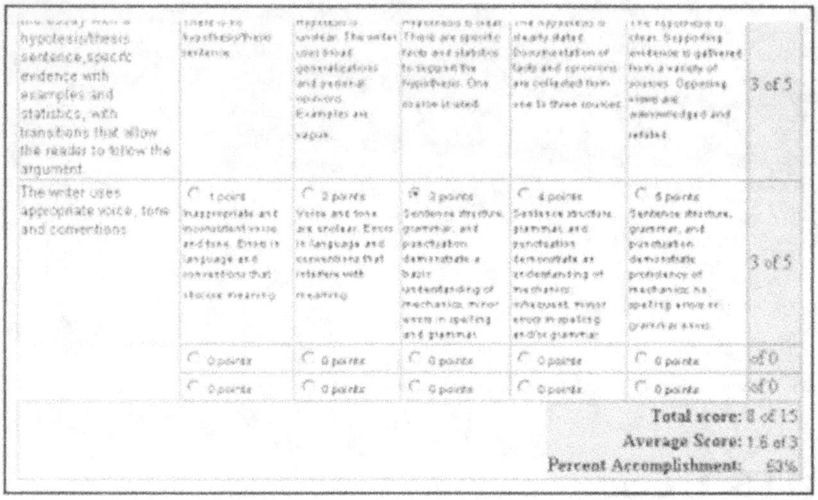

If the rubric is saved at the Rubric Builder site, the number of points scored on the rubric may be calculated.

Teacher Rubric Maker

The Teacher Rubric Maker is the simplest to use. However, the simplicity does limit the teacher's flexibility and creativity when creating a rubric. Basic items, such as the number of levels in the categories and the ratings, are pre-selected. The quality of the rubrics available varies greatly.

Figure 6.21: Rubric Generator

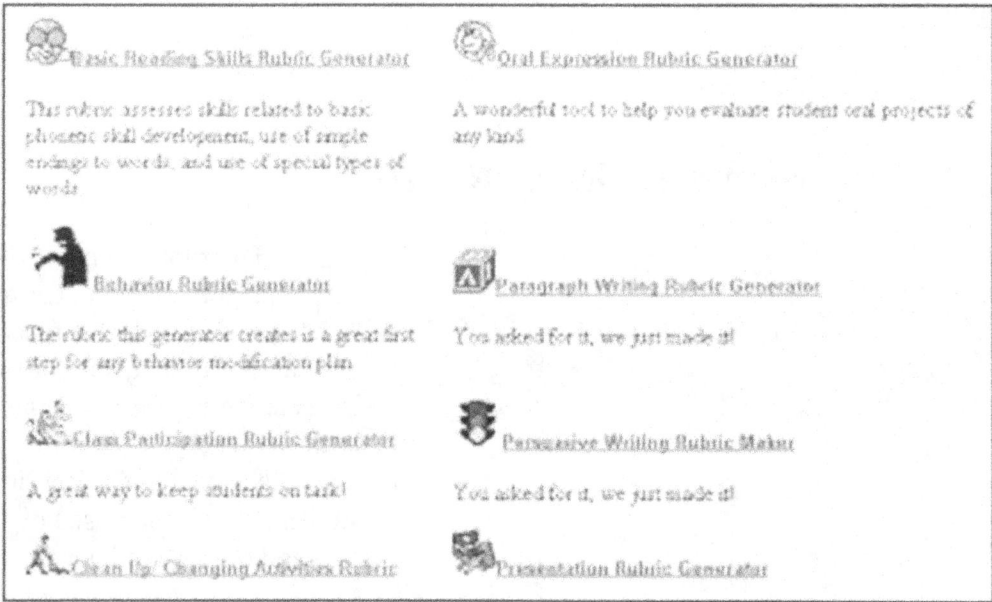

The Rubric Generator has more than 20 rubrics available. Click on the rubric that is wanted and the second screen gives you the option for inserting a picture.

Figure 6.22: Insert a Picture

After the picture is selected, the teacher clicks on the Generate Rubric Bar toward the bottom of the page.

Figure 6.23: Paragraph Writing Rubric

After the rubric is created, the teacher may print the rubric. It is possible to save the rubric by clicking the File menu, Save As command. The rubric saves nicely when the Web page option is chosen. If the teacher selects the Text file option, all formatting is lost.

Chapter 6: Making the Grade 117

Chapter 7

Search It! Using Search Engines Effectively

> *"What is the difference between exploring and being lost?"*
>
> *—Dan Eldon*

Seek and Ye Shall Find... Sometimes

The opening quote by Eldon sounds like the beginning of a bad joke. Thinking back to our history lessons, some of the greatest explorers were lost at least part of the time, and many made serendipitous discoveries that changed the world.

To many individuals, there is no great difference between being lost and exploration because both provide a certain measure of exhilaration and excitement mixed with anticipation and even some fear. Unfortunately, public schools do not share the same carefree approach to learning and student achievement for a variety of reasons. For one thing, the pressures and challenges facing educators do not leave much spare time for students to dilly-dally, let alone become lost.

When it comes to the uses of instructional technology, we want students to explore ideas and concepts and to create connections using critical thinking, but we certainly do not want to see valuable time wasted on ineffective, unstructured activities. When using technology, how do educators know what is good use of their time and the time of their students? What are the challenges and obstacles facing teachers who are planning for instruction with the intent of incorporating technology?

In this chapter we will discuss one critical aspect of technology integration, the search for information and how to make this experience more effective and useful for students and teachers.

Why Use Search Engines

Search engines, such as Google <http://www.google.com>, have become an integral part of how we both discover and uncover information that is available on the World Wide Web. The ability to effectively search for information has become so prevalent that there are literally hundreds, if not thousands, of recognized search engines each with their own special features and abilities. What are some of the reasons that educators use search engines? When we ask teachers this question, some of the common responses are:

- To have students do research
- To find background material for a lesson plan or online activity
- To find information of personal interest or information related to my job
- To see what's out there

Search engines offer the ability to quickly locate volumes of relevant information on a topic; however, there is a dark side. Search engines can also be mind-numbingly frustrating if not used effectively and efficiently. When following-up on the first question about why they use search engines, we then ask teachers for some reasons why they do not use search engines more often, either personally or with a class. See if these responses sound familiar.

- *I can never find what I am looking for.*
- *I am not sure which search engine to use.*
- *Are search engines safe to use with my class?*
- *There are too many advertisements.*
- *The information is irrelevant.*

The loudest and most common frustration is, **"Too many HITS!"**

There Is a Better Way

At this point, it is often beneficial to discuss with teachers some of the big differences between search engines. For example, there are several search engines that are not really search engines at all. Much of the time, teachers will find that they are actually searching in what is called a **directory**. Why does this matter? Well, directories, Yahoo <http://www.yahoo.com> being the best known, are similar to what we would see in a library. Topics are separated into major categorical headings, like *Business, Education, Reference*, etc.

Who determines the categories and what will go in them? People do. Directories are human driven. As a result, the scope of information is limited because it takes a while for humans to catalog the tens of thousands of Web sites created each year.

On the other hand, search engines, like Google <http://www.google.com>, tend to be much more powerful in their abilities to search the Web for information. One reason is that search engines employ special software programs that literally scour the Internet for Web sites and then collect them into massive databases. However, what good is all of this vast information if you cannot find what you need?

That is where training and knowledge come into play. If you become knowledgeable about how a specific search engine or directory works, then searching becomes a much more fruitful experience. We always suggest to teachers that they find one search engine, become familiar with all of the features that it offers and become an expert in using that one search engine. How do you decide what your "go to" search engine will be? We will make some suggestions. The table below is a starting point.

Comparison of Search Engines/Directories

Search Engines	Directories
➤ Maintain relatively large databases of Web sites ➤ Search using special software that continuously searches the Web for new and updated Web sites ➤ Generate large number of hits initially and provide advanced search features to narrow search ➤ Google is an example of a search engine	➤ Maintain relatively smaller databases of Web sites ➤ Are divided into broad categories catalogued by human beings ➤ Allow users to narrow a search fairly quickly by tunneling through the directory structure to find relevant information ➤ Yahoo is an example of a directory

There is no right or wrong way to go in making your decision. Depending on your needs, you might end up using a combination of search engines and directories.

Did You Say Google?

When it comes to searching the Web, the Google search engine is the tool of choice for millions of people worldwide. At the risk of sounding like an infomercial, we would like to highlight some of Google's unique features that make if stand out from the rest of the crowd. Here is why we use Google:

- It searches over two billion Web pages and returns results usually in less than one second.
- The user interface is extremely clean and easy to navigate.
- Google stores "snap shots" of every Web page that it visits; so if the page is unavailable, you can still see a version of the page when Google last visited it.
- Google offers an "I'm Feeling Lucky" button that takes you directly to your first hit, usually one that is right on target.
- Google allows you to set a filter to block inappropriate material.
- Google offers many powerful advanced search features, such as catalog searching, Web page translation, domain-specific searching, and similar page information to name a few.
- Google provides a free download called the Google Toolbar, which allows you to install Google as a toolbar right into your Internet browser.
- Advertisements are kept to a minimum and are not intrusive.

With the wide range of easy-to-use, advanced features, a clean interface, and significant search capability, it is not surprising why we choose to focus on using Google to learn how to search effectively.

Exhibit Center

The Google Interface

One advantage to using the Google search engine is the extremely user-friendly interface it offers. Advertisements do not clutter the screen. Pop-up screens are non-existent. What you see is a Web page with a simple design and no distractions. A look at the Google home page is shown below.

Figure 7.1: Google Home Page

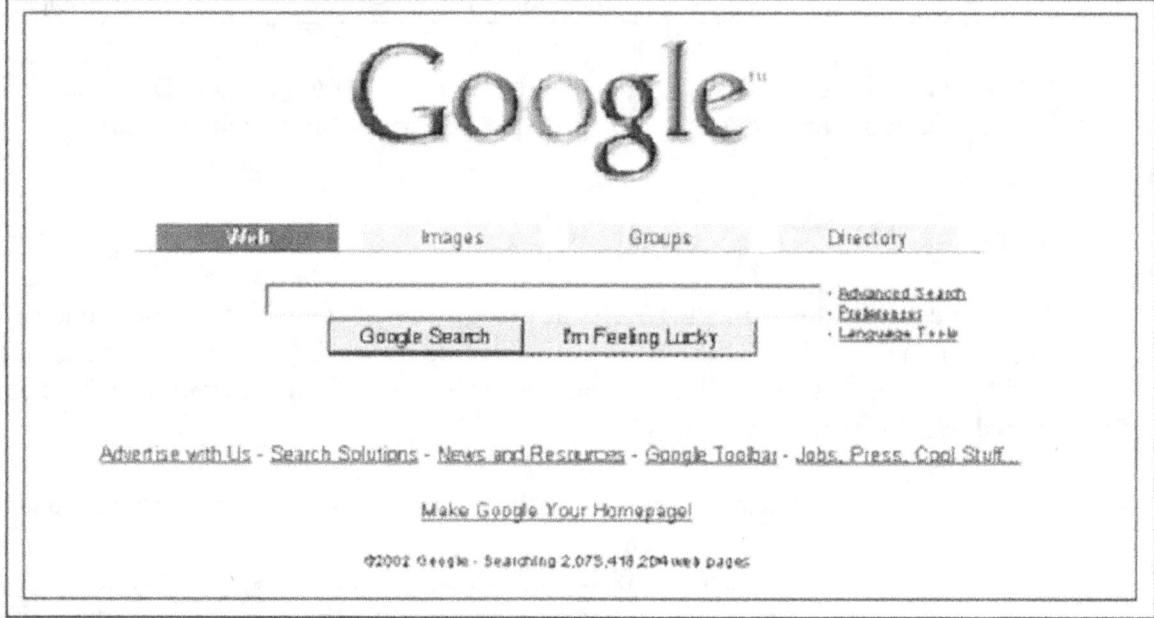

Like many search engines, a single box allows a person to type in a keyword or phrase for which to search. Google supports the use of advanced operators like quotes around keywords, the "plus" and "minus" signs as well others. The advanced search page <http://www.google.com/help/refinesearch.html> will provide everything that you need to know to help narrow a search. However, Google provides an easy-to-use form that includes many of these advanced features and makes learning them optional. We will show an example of this form and will provide directions on how to use it a little later in this chapter.

Google Snapshots

When it comes to searching the Internet, there are few things quite as frustrating as navigating to a site that you had bookmarked in your favorites, and for one reason or another, it is **gone**. Maybe the Web site is down for maintenance or maybe it just doesn't exist any longer.

Either way, you need the information contained on that site from the last time you visited it. There is no problem with Google. Thanks to Google's ability to cache Web sites, you can at least see how the site looked at the time Google most recently indexed it. For example, performing a search for Spartanburg School District 3, the following hits are returned.

Figure 7.2: Hits Returned by Google

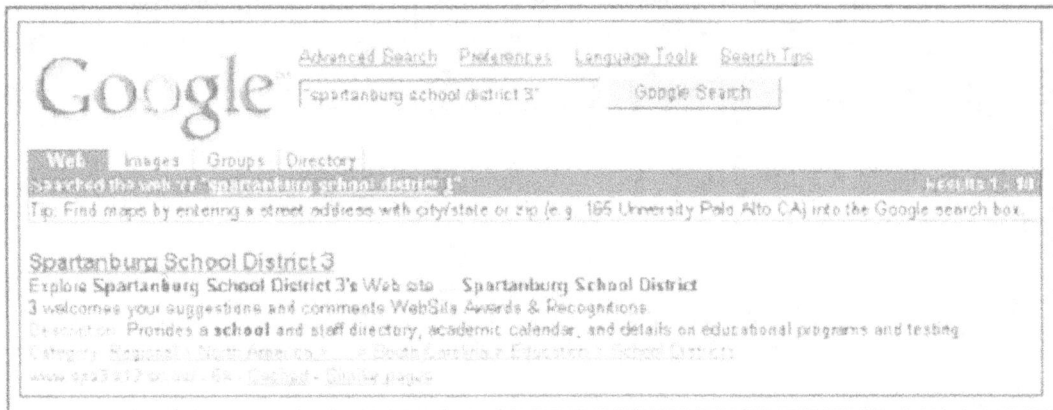

If I tried to follow the link to Spartanburg School District 3 Web site, and it was down for some reason, I could always click on the link near the end of the entry entitled Cached. Google would then display a screen similar to the following.

Figure 7.3: Cached Web Site

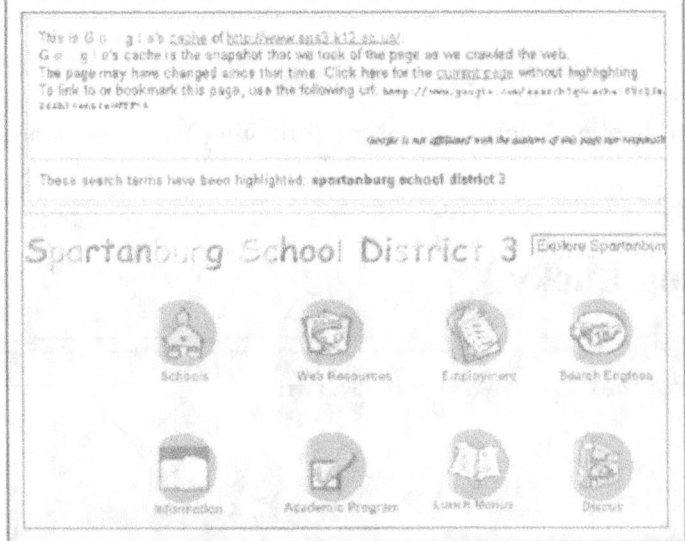

Google clearly indicates that the Web page displayed is a "snapshot" of the page as of the last time Google indexed it. Although the page may have been updated since then, at least this version is available in the event that the Web site is down.

I'm Feeling Lucky

Google provides the unique I'm Feeling Lucky button directly on the Google home page. For teachers on the go, the I'm Feeling Lucky button takes you directly to the first Web page that is returned from your search as opposed to displaying a list of hits returned. Because of Google's high success rate of returning relevant hits, this option will often take you to the information you need right away. For example, if I am conducting a search for Edgar Allen Poe and click on the search button, a list of hits, like the one below, appears.

Figure 7.4: Poe Hit List

Choosing to use the I'm Feeling Lucky button, the following Web page loaded immediately.

Figure 7.5: I'm Feeling Lucky

Safe Search Filtering

As educators, we are ultimately concerned with the safety and welfare of the children we teach. While the Internet offers the potential to expose students to new and exciting information not easily available before, it also exposes them to certain risks. Students, as well as any individual searching the Web, can inadvertently stumble upon inappropriate Web sites. By clicking on the Preferences link on the Google home page <http://www.google.com/preferences>, you can set the level of filtering Google will apply to searches.

Figure 7.6: Filtering Options

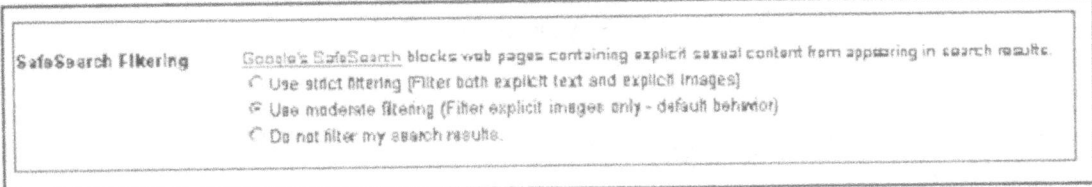

By default, Google is set to moderate filtering. That means it will automatically seek to block all explicit images. By changing the setting to strict filtering, both explicit text and images are blocked. No filtering is also an option. While Google acknowledges that no filtering system is perfect, it tries to limit exposure to inappropriate content by scouring the Web and through user suggestions and tips.

Google's Advanced Features

Despite Google's easy-to-use design and the "less is more" approach, this search engine offers an extremely powerful Advanced Search page that takes the guess work out of learning how to use advanced operators to narrow your search. To access the Advanced Search page, either click on the link with the same name or follow this link,<http://www.google.com/advanced_search>. The figure below is an example of the Advanced Search page prior to conducting a search.

Figure 7.7: Google Advanced Search Page

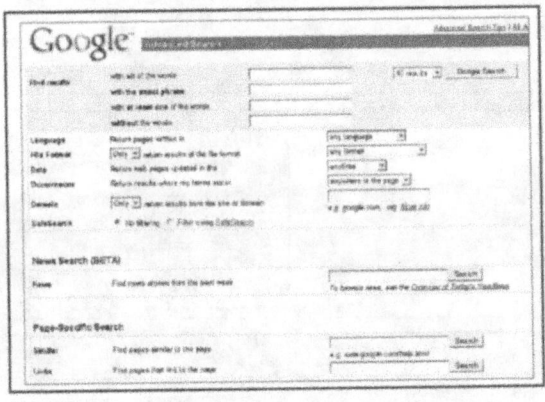

Near the top of the Advanced Search page in the **Find results** section, enter keywords or phrases and tell Google to search by **all** of the words, the **exact phrase, at least one of the words,** or **without** certain words. Rather than learn when to use a "+" or "-" operator, simply allow Google to do the hard work for you.

Figure 7.8: Find Results

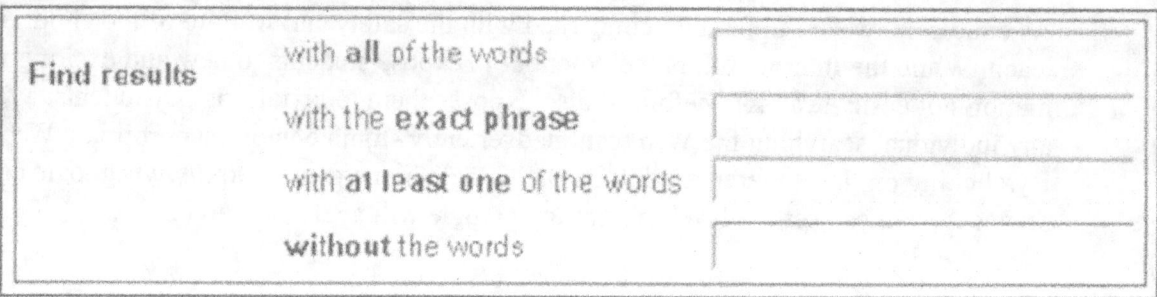

Google allows you to search for results written in one particular language. There are dozens of languages available from which to choose.

Figure 7.9: Language Search

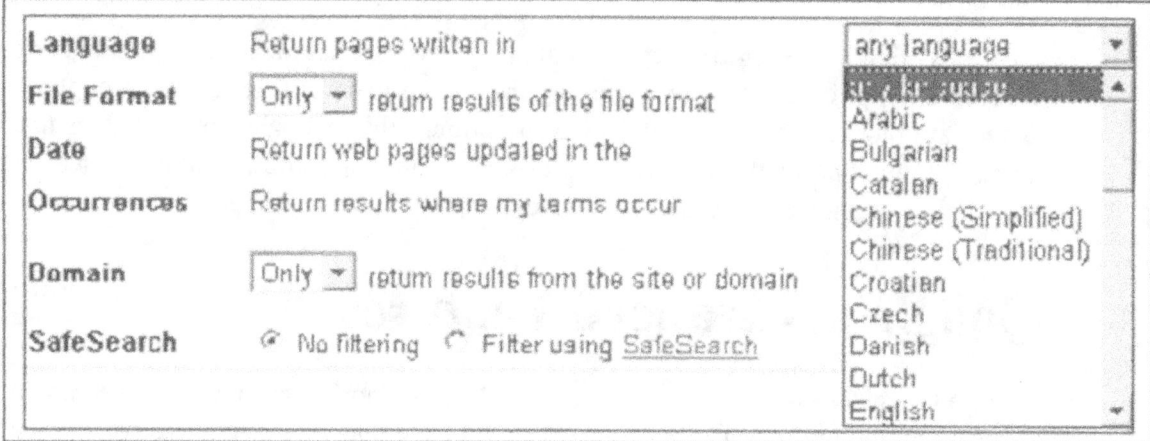

Also available on Google's advanced search page is the ability to search by a specific file format (i.e., Microsoft Word document, PowerPoint presentation, etc.).

Another extremely useful feature is the **Date** search. The Date search allows you to filter for content on the basis of whether it has been updated within in the past three months, past six months, or past year.

Figure 7.10: Date Search

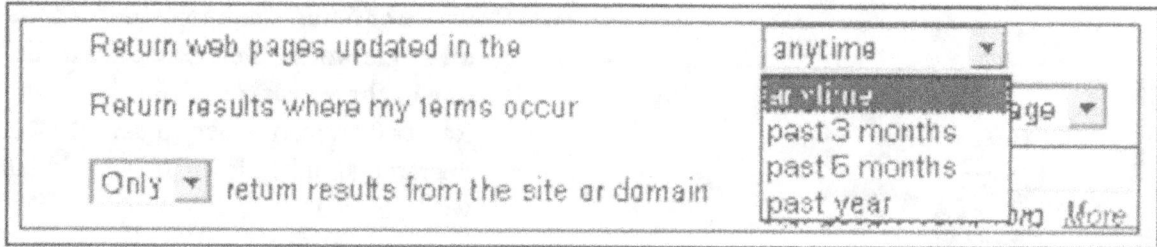

The **Occurrences** field enables you to narrow a search by specifying in what portion of the page your search term must appear (i.e., in the title of the page, in the text of the page, etc.).

Figure 7.11: Occurrences Search

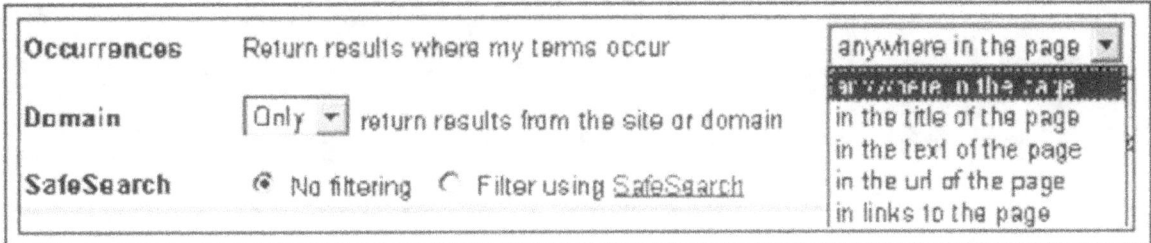

The **Domain** search field is useful because it narrows down your search to one specific Web site. Although many sites provide their own search capabilities, using Google's **Domain** search feature often yields more relevant results than the Web site's own search engine.

The last feature to mention on the Advanced Search page is the **News Search** feature. This feature allows you to search for news headlines within the past week. It is a very handy feature when looking for specific, timely information.

Figure 7.12: News Search

The Google Toolbar

Using Google's powerful search features is made even more convenient by installing the Google Toolbar. By installing this very small application to your Internet Browser (Microsoft Internet Explorer 5.x or higher), one can search the Internet using Google without ever navigating to the Google Web site. Here's how it works.

- Navigate to the Google Web site <http://www.google.com>
- Click on the Google Toolbar Link <http://toolbar.google.com/>

Figure 7.13: Google Toolbar Link

- The Google Toolbar download page will load.
- Read the information about the toolbar and proceed down the page to the **Select Your Language** section.
- Select the appropriate language.
- Review the **System Requirements**:
    - Microsoft Windows 95/98/ME/NT/2000/XP
    - Microsoft Internet Explorer version 5 or later

Figure 7.14: System Requirements and Language Selection

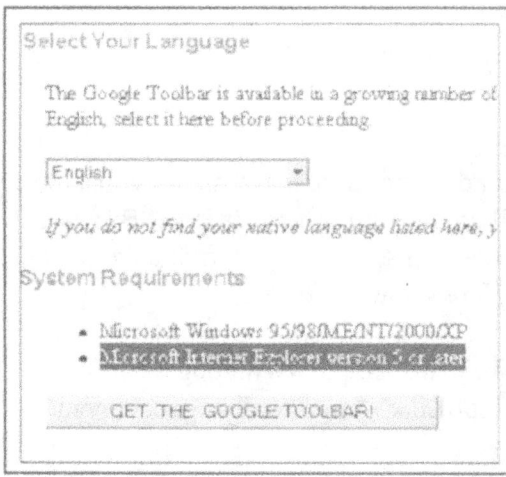

- Click one time on the **GET THE GOOGLE TOOLBAR!** Button.
- Read the Terms of Use by following the link by the same name.
- Click on the button that says **I Agree to the Terms of Use—Install the Google Toolbar**.

Figure 7.15: Install the Google Toolbar

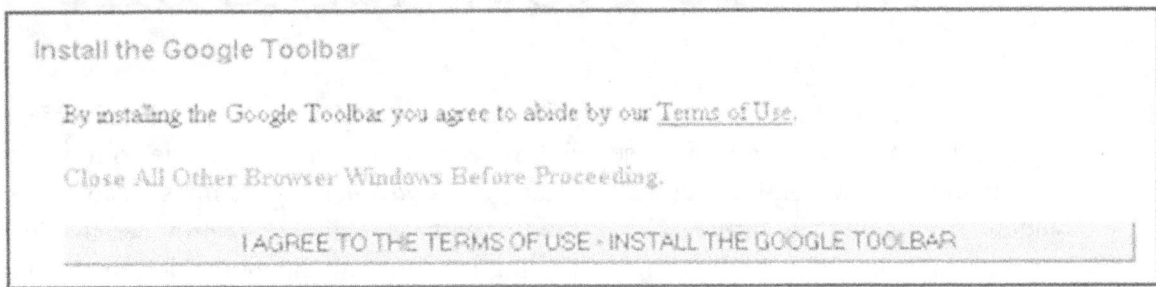

Choose whether to install Google with or without the advanced features described in the **Choose Configuration** screen.

- The Google Toolbar will then be automatically installed and ready for use.

Figure 7.16: The Google Toolbar

Show Me How It's Done

When showing teachers how to use the Google search engine, it would be convenient to simply ask them to read the advanced search tips section <http://www.google.com/help/refine-search.html>. However, the fact that it is labeled as *advanced* sometimes discourages individuals from going any further. This is not to say that the directions provided by Google are not extremely useful and effective, but finding the time and the motivation to read the material may not be possible. Instead, we take the hands-on approach and walk teachers through an actual example of searching using the Advanced Search page in Google. There are several goals we keep in mind when doing this exercise.

1. Demonstrate Google's ability to find highly relevant information.
2. Show how to narrow a search from an overwhelming number of results to a much smaller, manageable number.
3. Demonstrate the ease of using Google's built-in advanced search functions instead of requiring the individual to provide the appropriate syntax.

The Search Is On

In the following example, we will show you how to take a search that is too broad and unwieldy to one that is more narrow and focused. In the example, we will be searching for information on the American author, Edgar Allan Poe. First we will start by navigating to the Advanced Search page <http://www.google.com/advanced_search?hl=en> by clicking on the link by the same name on the Google home page. Once the page loads, we type the search term *edgar allan poe* in the **with all of the words** search field in the **Find results** section. Notice that the keywords are all entered in lowercase letters. Entering the keywords using uppercase letters will cause Google to restrict your search to results that only contain the keywords in uppercase, excluding lowercase results. On the other hand, entering keywords using lowercase letters will yield results that contain the keywords in both uppercase and lowercase forms.

Figure 7.17: Searching With All of the Words

Find results	with **all** of the words	edgar allan poe
	with the **exact phrase**	
	with **at least one** of the words	
	without the words	

This search is constructed very broadly and results in 212,000 hits. This is because, under these conditions, Google is searching for the keywords in every possible combination. By typing the same keywords in the **with the exact phrase** field and then performing the search, the results drop down to 193,000. This is still probably too many to look through during a planning period. This time, notice that when the first page of results loads, Google has added the appropriate operators to your original keywords. In this case, Google has inserted quotation marks at the beginning and at the end of the keywords.

Figure 7.18: Google Inserts Quotation Operator

![Google search box with "edgar allan poe"]

To continue narrowing the search, we will enter *annabel lee* in the with **at least one of the words** field while keeping edgar allan poe in the **with the exact phrase** field. This search results in 52,100 hits. This search was much more restrictive because it required all results to contain at least the words *annabel* or *lee*. This is the syntax that Google creates from your query.

Figure 7.19: Syntax for at Least One of the Words

![Google search box with: annabel OR lee "edgar allan poe"]

Now we will enter the keyword *raven* in the **without the words** field. This will exclude any results that contain the keyword *raven*.

Figure 7.20: Without the Words Field

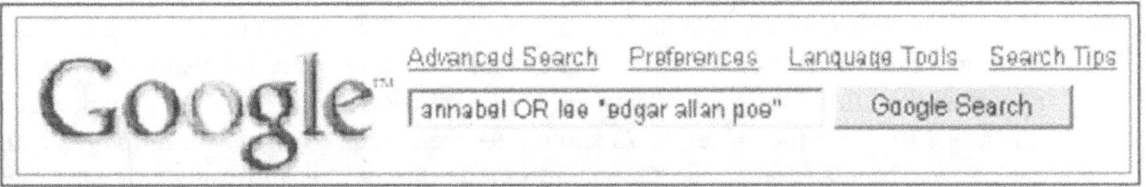

Find results	with **all** of the words	
	with the **exact phrase**	edgar allan poe
	with **at least one** of the words	annabel lee
	without the words	raven

Chapter 7: Search It! Using Search Engines Effectively **131**

The number of hits is now down to 50,200. If we then specify that Google only return results written in a specific language, the number of hits again declines (i.e., specifying *Spanish* results in 781 hits).

Another useful search technique that enables you to narrow down the number of results is to use the **File Format** search field. In this example, we will specify results that only contain Microsoft Word file formats.

Figure 7.21: File Format Search Field

[Search form showing: Find results with all of the words (blank), with the exact phrase "edgar allan poe", with at least one of the words "annabel lee", without the words "raven"; Language: any language; File Format: Only return results of the file format Microsoft Word (.doc); 10 results]

The number of hits drops down to 79.

We then reset the **File Format** field to *any format* and the **Language** field to *any language* to make the search appropriately broad before using some other advanced search fields.

Making use of the **Date** search field usually decreases the number of hits significantly because Google is only searching for pages updated in the past 3–12 months depending upon your specifications.

The **Occurrences** search field allows you to narrow a search by specifying where the keywords must appear on a page. In the example we have specified that the keywords must appear in the title of the page. Using the **Occurrences** search field drops the number of hits down to 130. If we then reset the **Occurrences** field back to *anywhere in the page* and specify a particular domain for Google to search, the number of results will again decrease.

Figure 7.22: Occurrences Field

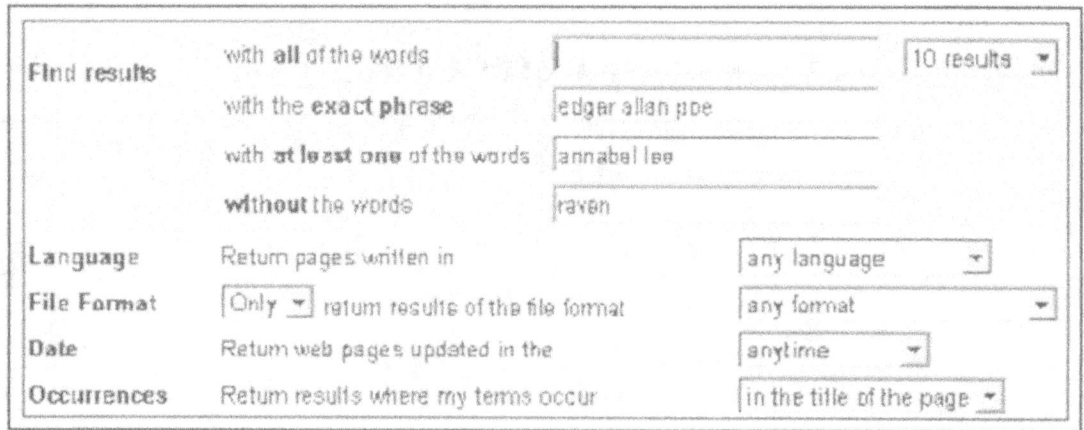

Using the same keyword combinations in the **Find results** section and specifying *eapoe.org* in the **Domain** search field, the number of results drops down to 48. This occurred because Google was searching the *eapoe.org* domain, and only this domain, using the keywords provided.

Figure 7.23: Domain Search

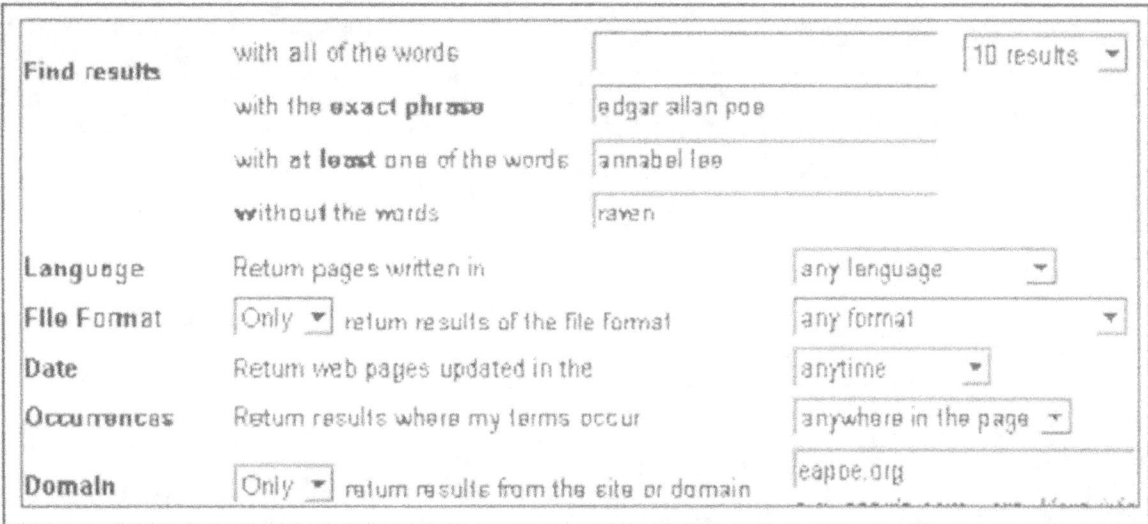

This section did not cover all of the advanced search features available using Google. Take a few minutes of your time and explore on your own. The advanced search features are certainly worth exploring and will certainly save you time in the long run.

Chapter 7: Search It! Using Search Engines Effectively 133

Chapter 8

What's Next?

> *"The goal is to create a learning experience that arouses and sustains children's curiosity, enriching their capacities and responding to their questions in ways that are deeply engaging."*
> —*Alfie Kohn*

This book begins by posing the question: *"Which productivity tips would have the most impact in facilitating student learning?"* After all, students are the reason that teachers do what they do. Planning, constructing, and facilitating student learning occupy major portions of a teacher's time.

A teacher's life can be overwhelming. Teachers must design lessons, plan instruction, grade papers—on personal time, not company time. At school teachers must deliver instruction, calm student angst, assess learning, handle student disagreements, write curriculum, contact parents, and smile.

Struggling to Stay Above Water

But, if teachers are struggling with all of the classroom management issues (*trying to stay above water*), doesn't that affect student learning? Put it this way—if a teacher is struggling to keep track of bookmarks or is grappling with using assessment tools, doesn't that keep the teacher's focus away from the student?

If we mire down in the detailed steps of figuring out things for the student to do, we tend to lose the big picture of how or what the student is learning. In other words, by focusing on details, we tend to make the parts bigger than the whole. We need to change that around.

Making the Whole Bigger than Its Parts

Developing well-crafted, instructionally enriching, project-based lessons is a mighty task. Focusing on the whole, instead of the separate parts of the lesson, enables us to ask the important questions: *Are students actively engaged in learning? Do they understand what they are supposed to know and be able to do at the end of the lesson? Do students know why they are learning what they are learning?*

This is not to question the dedication of teachers. We know that teachers are motivated to improve learning opportunities and to model instructional excellence. Instructional leaders need to acknowledge that hard work. Teachers need to be rewarded for their innovation, their ability to change, and their continued growth.

The Same Way of Thinking

The old way of thinking about curriculum and instruction was to give the teacher the textbook and "Bam!" student learning took place.

The new way of thinking is equally distressing and frightfully familiar. The new way of thinking is that computers and software could be given to teachers and, "Bam!" high-quality lessons, that engage and challenge students, would emerge.

Misguided Effort

It is only with the benefit of hindsight that we can see that that effort was misguided. One of the major obstacles was the sheer amount of time needed to make technology integration take place. Another equally imposing obstacle was teacher frustration. URLs disappeared. The technology didn't work. The Web was slow. The everyday hassle of using technology became an obstacle by itself.

Oh me, oh my, what is a teacher to do? Some teachers did what sensible people have done since the beginning of time. They avoided the frustration and stopped depending upon the technology. Technology was not for them to use.

Other teachers struggled to use technology regularly. These teachers created new material and discovered new ways of looking at information. These early users demonstrated conclusively that teachers have the willingness and capacity to develop quality Web-based projects.

Taming the Technology

Media specialists inherited the responsibility of helping teachers integrate technology into the curriculum. They too struggled mightily, but gamely, assisting teachers as they developed project-based Web lessons.

Administrators recognized early that if teachers were to integrate technology into student experiences, then they needed adequate technology, tremendous support, and lots of encouragement. What wasn't recognized was the time and effort that it would take.

In part, media specialists inherited the job of technology trainer because the training was perceived to be a one-shot deal. Teach teachers to use technology and move on to something else.

Who thought that technology training would be a continuous process? Technology trainers and media specialists (oftentimes both roles occupied by the same person) spend an inordinate amount of time learning and relearning the use of technology tools. We sometimes fail to recognize that technology, as a skill set, is a moving target. It is not surprising that we are struggling. If media specialists or technology trainers are to support teachers, they need to be provided with the time to provide the training.

The task, although daunting, is important. Schools, the centers for their communities, level the playing field and provide equity and access to all children. Students who have computers and Internet connectivity available in the home have greater access to information and to success. By providing technology in the schools, we lessen the impact of the digital divide.

Energize, Refresh, and Renew

The whole point of becoming more productive and saving time is to increase opportunities for students to learn. We dream about tomorrow. We envision the classrooms that can be someday.

Classrooms of the future are noisy places. It's a joyful mélange of excitement and collegiality. Working together, students solve problems and brainstorm. They communicate regularly with each other and outside audiences. They are good communicators. Accustomed to having an audience every day and communicating information in ways that people will understand, students are comfortable manipulating information and molding it into something new and wonderful. They take risks.

Through the use of the timesaving applications available on the Web and other technology, teachers have an opportunity to engage students in new ways. As we are able to manage the technology better, the use of technology will grow and improve in effectiveness and efficiency. By using cooperative learning strategies and assessing how well students interact and perform using group problem-solving skills, we can design rubrics that assess those performance skills.

Competent and Committed Teachers

Technology in the hands of a savvy teacher engages students. Through a technology-rich classroom, students are provided access to information resources that are key to the pursuit of knowledge. Solving problems and making informed decisions—authentic learning experiences—engage students in what life is like in the real world. By making these connections to the real world and by holding students accountable for these connections through rubrics and interactive exercise makers, we emphasize the importance of learning. Students locate, evaluate, and collect information from a variety of sources through technology-enhanced research tools. In the technology-rich classroom, students will be engage in problem-based simulations and experiences that connect to their local communities.

We all know the skills necessary for a student to be successful in the modern age. As Alvin Toffler said, "The illiterate of the 21st century will not be those who cannot read and write, but those who cannot learn, unlearn, and relearn." What better summation of the power of technology than being able to learn, unlearn, and relearn—in nanoseconds it seems.

Appendix: Source List

Chapter 1

Bloom's Taxonomy figure created using **Inspiration**—<www.inspiration.com>

Chapter 2

Internet Explorer—<www.microsoft.com/windows/ie/default.asp>
Backflip—<www.backflip.com> (All Backflip logos, graphics, and content are the property of Backflip, Inc., and are copyrighted. All Backflip logos, graphics, and content are reprinted with permission of Backflip, Inc.)
Netscape—<www.netscape.com> (Netscape browser window © 2002 Netscape Communications Corporation. Used with permission. Netscape Communications has not authorized, sponsored, endorsed, or approved this publication and is not responsible for its content.)
iKeepBookmarks—<www.ikeepbookmarks.com>
MyBookmarks—<www.mybookmarks.com>
CrystalPort—<www.crystalport.com>
Opera—<www.opera.com>

Chapter 3

Inspiration—<www.inspiration.com> (All diagrams and templates in Chapter 3 are created with Inspiration® or reprinted from Inspiration templates.)
Kidspiration—<www.kidspiration.com> (Kidspiration is published by Inspiration.)

Chapter 4

Hot Potatoes—<www.halfbakedsoftware.com> or <web.uvic.ca/hrd/hotpot/> (Screen shots of Hot Potatoes by permission of Half-Baked Software, Inc.)
WebPractest—<http://www.wm.edu/CAS/modlang/gasmit/webpractest/> (Screen shots of WebPractest by permission of Gary A. Smith.)
Interactive Exercise Maker—<http://makers.cet.middlebury.edu/makers/index.htm> (Screen Shots by Tricollege Mellon Language Project at Haverford, Bryn Mawr, and Swarthmore colleges by Dan Beeby.)

Chapter 5

Worksheet Generator — <http://school.discovery.com/teachingtools/worksheetgenerator/index.html> (Screen Shots by permission of DiscoverySchool.com.)
PuzzleMaker — <http://www.puzzlemaker.com/>. (Screen Shots by permission of DiscoverySchool.com.)
Web Tools for Educators — <http://www.teach-nology.com/web_tools/>
Bingo Maker Generator — <http://www.teach-nology.com/web_tools/>
Personal Educational Press — <http://www.educationalpress.org/educationalpress/Index.asp>
The Learning Page — <http://www.learningpage.com>
SuperKids Math Worksheet Generator — <http://www.superkids.com/aweb/tools/math/>
A+ Math — <http://www.aplusmath.com>

Chapter 6

RubiStar — <http://rubistar.4teachers.org/> (Screen Shots by permission of High Plains RTEC, University of Kansas.)
ClassWeb Rubric Builder — <http://www.landmark-project.com/classweb/tools/rubric_builder.php3>
Teacher Rubric Maker — <http://teachers.teach-nology.com/web_tools/rubrics/>

Chapter 7

Google — <http:www.google.com>

Index

A

A Journey Through Poe (Figure) 60
A Profile of China (Figure) 53
A Saved Rubric (Figure). 115
A+ Math—http://www.aplusmath.com 87, 140
Add Bookmark Window (Figure). 23
Add Text (Figure) 73
Adding a Bookmark to Backflip (Figure) 27
Adding a Favorite (Figure) 21
Adding a Folder to Bookmarks (Figure) 23
Adding a Folder to Favorites (Figure) 22
Adding a New Bookmark Button (Figure). 29
Adding a New Bookmark
    to iKeepBookmarks (Figure) 29
Adding a New Folder Button (Figure) 28
Adding a New Folder Screen (Figure) 28
Adding a Tab from Favorites (Figure) 30
Adding Clues (Figure) 78
Adding Ideas (Figure). 45
Adding Reading Text 73
Adding Text 73
Adding Text to a Symbol 44
Advanced Maze Creation (Figure) 98
American Literature Example (Figure) 76
American Memory Collection 10
American Writers (Figure) 62
American Writers Series (Figure) 63
American Writers—Matching (Figure) 62
An Aquarium Ecosystem (Figure) 53
Animal Maze Collection (Figure) 97
Animal Survival Guided Tour (Figure) 41
Applications Are Easy To Use 59
Assessment 101–117
Assessment Tools to Improve Classroom
    Instruction. 55–80

B

Backflip—www.backflip.com. 8, 14, 24–27, 139
Backflip Login (Figure) 24
Backflip Management Menu (Figure) 26
Backflip Navigation Menu (Figure) 25
Backflipping Bookmarks (Figure) 17
Background Using Inspiration 39
Beeby, Don 65
Berlioz, Hector Louis 1
Bingo Maker 85
Bingo Maker Generator (Figure) 85
Bingo Maker Generator—
    http://www.teach-nology.com/web_tools/ 140
Bloom's taxonomy 6, 7
Bloom's Taxonomy (Figure). 7
Bookmarking with IKeepBookmarks (Figure). 17
Bookmarking with Internet Explorer 14
Bookmarking with MyBookmarks (Figure). 18
Bookmarking with Netscape 16
Bookmarks 8
Bookmarks & Tabs 8, 12
Bookmarks in iKeepBookmarks (Figure) 28
Bookmarks Menu (Figure) 22
Brace Map 34
Brace Map (Figure) 35
Brainstorming Animal Survival Needs (Figure) 42
Brainstorming Basic Needs of
    Animals Unit (Figure) 41
Brainstorming Causes of Weather (Figure) 42
Brainstorming Results of Harvesting
    the Rain Forest (Figure) 40
Brainstorming the Causes of the American
    Civil War (Figure). 37
Bridge Map. 34
Bubble Map 34
Building a Rubric with ClassWeb Rubric
    Builder (Figure) 113

C

Cached Web Site (Figure). 123
Calculating Score (Figure) 116
Causes & Impact of the American Civil War
    (Figure). 38
Changes in a Teacher's Role 7
Changing Symbol's Appearance. 47
Changing the Classroom 5
Characteristics of a Rabbit (Figure) 52
Circle Map 34
Clarify Thinking 34

ClassWeb 104
ClassWeb Rubric Builder 9
ClassWeb Rubric Builder (Figure) 105
ClassWeb Rubric Builder—
    http://www.landmark-project.com/classweb/
    tools/rubric_builder.php3 140
Click on Potato (Figure) 71
ClozeMaker 65
Comparison of Search Engines/Directories 121
Completed Objectives (Figure) 114
Completed Rubric (Figure) 112
Completing Your Rubric (Figure) 114
Continents (Figure) 45
Cool Mazes (Figure) 97
Copying or Printing Your Puzzle 98
Create a Matching Quiz Using Word Lists (Figure) . . 96
Create a Worksheet (Figure) 94
Create Puzzles Online (Figure) 98
Creating a Gap (Figure) 80
Creating a Link (Figure) 46
Creating a New Folder in Backflip (Figure) 26
Creating a Worksheet Using Puzzlemaker
    Vocabulary Lists 96
Creating Bookmarks with Internet Explorer 20
Creating Bookmarks with Netscape 22
Creating Flash Cards 100
Creating Other Mazes 97
Creating Other Puzzles 98
Creating Saved Window Setups with
    Opera Web Browser 31
Creating Tab Groups with CrystalPort
    Web Browser 29
Crossword Grid (Figure) 78
Crossword Puzzle (Figure) 57
CrystalPort Browser Tab Group (Figure) 18
CrystalPort Web Browser 12, 18, 29
CrystalPort—
    www.crystalport.com 139

D

Date Search (Figure) 126
Desktop (Figure) 69
DHTML Makers 65
Dialogue Box (Figure) 73
DictoMaker 65
Did You Say Google? 121
Directories 120

Discovery School's Worksheet Generator (Figure) . . . 94
Domain Search (Figure) 133
Double Bubble Map 34, 35
Double Bubble Map (Figure) 36
Downloads (Figure) 67
Dynamic HTML 65

E

Eldon, Dan 119
Elements of the Periodic Table: Matching Quiz 89
Elements of the Periodic Table: Word Scramble 88
Enhancing Instruction 82
Entering Words in a Grid (Figure) 85
EvalMaker 65
Ewing, Sam 81
Example of Clozemaker (Figure) 66
Example of EvalMaker (Figure) 66
Example of MatchMaker (Figure) 66
Example of MultiMaker (Figure) 66
Examples of Assessment Materials on the Web 60
Examples of Inspiration as a Classroom Tool 40
Exhibit Center 10
Exhibit Center (Assessment Tools) 60
Exhibit Center (Bookmarks & Tabs) 14
Exhibit Center (Inspiration) 40
Exhibit Center (Rubrics) 106
Exhibit Center (Search Engines) 122
Exhibit Center (Worksheet Generators) 88
Expanding a Folder (Figure) 15
Exploring Impact of Deforestation (Figure) 40

F

F O I L 83
Favorites Window (Figure) 21
Favorites Button (Figure) 14, 20
Favorites Menu (Figure) 14
File Download (Figure) 68
File Format Search Field (Figure) 132
Filtering Options (Figure) 125
Find Results (Figure) 126
Flash Card Selection (Figure) 100

G

Gapped Words Alternative (Figure) 80
Getting Started (Assessments) 67
Getting Started with a Kidspiration Diagram 51
Giraudoux, Jean 101

Google. 119–133
Google Advanced Search Page (Figure). 125
Google Home Page (Figure). 122
Google Inserts Quotation Operator (Figure) 131
Google Snapshots. 122
Google Toolbar Link (Figure) 128
Google's Advanced Features. 125
Google—
    http:www.google.com. 140
Guided Tour 60

H

Hits Returned by Google (Figure) 123
Hot Potatoes 9, 55–63, 67–80
Hot Potatoes Homepage (Figure). 67
Hot Potatoes Short Cut (Figure). 71
Hot Potatoes—www.halfbakedsoftware.com 139
Hotlists 1
HTML Code (Figure) 115
Hyerle, David 34

I

I Don't Have Time to Think 1–3
I'm Feeling Lucky 124
I'm Feeling Lucky (Figure) 124
iKeepBookmarks 8
iKeepBookmarks—
    www.ikeepbookmarks.com. 139
Improving Technology-Based Instruction with
    Bookmarks & Tabs. 12
Information Box (Figure). 75
Insert a New Symbol 45
Insert a Picture (Figure) 117
Insert Picture (Figure) 74
Inserting a Picture. 74
Inspiration Screen (Figure). 44
Inspiration—
    http://www.inspiration.com 139
Inspiration. 9, 33–53
Install the Google Toolbar (Figure) 129
Interactive Exercise Maker at Swarthmore
    College (Figure) 65
Interactive Exercise Maker—
    http://makers.cet.middlebury.edu/makers/
    index.htm 139
Interactive Exercise Makers 65–67
Internet Explorer. 14

Internet Explorer—
    www.microsoft.com/windows/ie/default.asp . . . 139

J

JBC 58
JBC Screen (Figure) 72
JCloze 57
JCloze (Figure) 79
JCross 57
JCross (Figure) 78
JMatch 58
JMatch (Figure) 79
JMix 58
JMix (Figure) 77
JMix Example (Figure). 77
JQuiz 58
JQuiz (Figure). 76

K

Kidspiration 9, 51–53
Kidspiration Opening Screen (Figure). 51
Kidspiration Screen (Figure) 51
Kidspiration—www.kidspiration.com 139
Knowledge Bowl 82
Kohn, Alfie. 135

L

Lab Equipment (Figure) 58
Landmark Project 104
Language Search (Figure) 126
Learning Page 86
Link (Figure). 46
Linking Symbols 45
Looking in a Folder (Figure) 15

M

Main Idea (Figure) 44
Maintaining a Focus on Student Achievement. 6
Making the Grade. 101–118
Making the Whole Bigger than Its Parts 135
Making Your Category Selections (Figure) 111
Masher 58
MatchMaker 65
Media Specialist 2, 136
Milne, A. A. 11
Mixed-Up Sentence (Figure) 63
Mnemonic device 6

Multi-flow Map 34
MultiMaker. 65
Multimedia Project Rubric (Figure). 110
Multiple-Choice Quiz (Figure). 58
My Folders in Backflip (Figure). 25
MyBookmarks—www.mybookmarks.com 139

N

Netscape 16
Netscape Sidebar (Figure) 16
Netscape—www.netscape.com. 139
New Timesaving Features. 12
News Search (Figure). 127
"No Child Left Behind" Act of 2001 6
Notes on Using Kidspiration 51

O

Occurrences Field (Figure). 132
Occurrences Search (Figure) 127
One Click Does It. 97
Opening a Template 49
Opening a Template (Figure). 49
Opera 12, 14, 18, 19
Opera—
    www.opera.com 139
Options for Saving Your Worksheet (Figure) 96
Organize It: Managing Bookmarks 11–32
Other Interactive Exercise Makers 64

P

Paragraph Writing Rubric (Figure) 117
Performance Indicators. 104, 113
Personal Educational Express. 86, 99
Personal Educational Press—
    http://www.educationalpress.org/
    educationalpress/Index.asp 140
Persuasive Essay Rubric 108
Persuasive Essay Rubric (Figure). 115
Plato 5
Poe Hit List (Figure). 124
Poe, Edgar Allan. 60
Poe's "Annabel Lee" (Figure). 61
Poe's Biographical Information (Figure) 61
Print Your Worksheet (Figure) 95
Printing Or Saving the Rubric (Figure) 111
PuzzleMaker. 84
PuzzleMaker Examples (Figure) 84
PuzzleMaker—
    http://www.puzzlemaker.com/ 140

R

RapidFire (Figure) 46
RapidFire Diagram (Figure). 47
Rating Scale (Figure) 110
Rating Scale Criteria (Figure) 111
Ready-To-Go Worksheets (Figure). 84
Review of Poetry Terms (Figure) 60
Rogers, Will 55
RubiStar 9, 103
RubiStar (Figure) 109
RubiStar—
    http://rubistar.4teachers.org/ 140
Rubric Builder Start Page (Figure). 113
Rubric Generator (Figure) 115
Rubric Maker 9, 103, 105, 116
Rubric on Edgar Allan Poe Report. 106
Rubric Samples (Figure). 109
Rubric Samples from Rubric Generator (Figure). . . 105
Rubrics 9, 101–117

S

Safe Search Filtering 125
Sample Bingo Board from Personal Educational
    Press (Figure) 93
Sample Flash Cards (Back) from Personal
    Educational Press (Figure) 92
Sample Flash Cards (Front) from Personal
    Educational Press (Figure) 91
Sample Quiz from Personal Educational
    Press (Figure) 90
Sample Topics on RubiStar (Figure) 104
Save As (Figure). 68
Saving a Custom Template 50
Saving a Diagram as a Template (Figure) 50
Saving Favorites to a Floppy Disk 19
Saving Files (Figure) 74
Saving Time 5–10
Saving Your Files 75
Saving Your Worksheet. 95
Search Engines 120
Search It! Using Search Engines Effectively . . . 119–134
Search Techniques 10, 119–134
Searching With All of the Words (Figure) 130
Selecting a Template (Figure). 49

Selecting the Output Style (Figure) 99
Selecting Word Lists (Figure). 86
Self-Extractor (Figure) 69
Setup (Figure). 69
Setup Wizard (Figure) 70
Show Me How It's Done 10
Show Me How It's Done (Assessment Tools) 67
Show Me How It's Done (Bookmarks & Tabs) 20
Show Me How It's Done (Inspiration) 43
Show Me How It's Done (Rubrics) 109
Show Me How It's Done (Search Engines) 130
Show Me How It's Done (Worksheet Generators). . . . 94
Simple Steps. 8
Steps To Creating An Exercise 72
Study Sheet Options (Figure). 100
SuperKids Math Worksheet Generator. 87
SuperKids Math Worksheet Generator—
    http://www.superkids.com/aweb/tools/math/ . . . 140
Symbol Palette (Figure) 48
Syntax For At Least One of the Words (Figure) 131
System Requirements and Language
    Selection (Figure). 128

T

Tab Advantages. 12, 13
Tab groups 12
Tab Toolbar (Figure) 30
Tabs. 8, 18
Teacher Rubric Maker—
    http://teachers.teach-nology.com/
    web_tools/rubrics/ 140
Teacher Rubric Maker 105, 116
Teaching To The Test 102
Template to Organize Knowledge on the Civil War . . . 37
The "I Have A Dream Speech" (Figure) 62
The Diary of Anne Frank 55
The Disappearing URL 10
The Google Interface 122
The Google Toolbar 127
The Google Toolbar (Figure) 129
The Learning Page 86
The Learning Page—
    http://www.learningpage.com. 140
The Listen Button (Figure). 52
The Netscape Bookmarks Menu (Figure) 16
The Same Way of Thinking 136
The Search Is On 130

The Six Applications 57
There Is A Better Way 120
Thinking Maps 34
Thinking with Bubbles. 33–54
Thinking-Idea Map Template (Figure). 36
Three Tools To Develop Rubrics 103
Tiled Windows in Opera Software Web
    Browser (Figure). 19
Toffler, Alvin 137
Tree Map. 34
Tricollege Mellon Language Project 65
Tutorials (Figure) 112

U

University of Victoria 56
Using Backflip to Manage Bookmarks Online 24
Using ClassWeb Rubric Builder. 112
Using Graphics (Figure). 48
Using Hot Potatoes To Create Quizzes 70
Using iKeepBookmarks to Manage Favorites Online . 27
Using JBC. 72
Using JCloze. 79
Using JCross. 78
Using JMatch 79
Using JMix 77
Using JQuiz 76
Using RapidFire 46
Using RapidFire (Figure) 47
Using RubiStar 109
Using Rubrics To Define Instruction 102
Using Worksheet Generator 94

V

Valery, Paul. 33
Viewing Tabs in Tile Mode (Figure) 30
Vocabulary Lists and Answer Lists (Figure) 99

W

War of 1812 55
Web Page File (Figure). 75
Web Tools for Educators 85
Web Tools for Educators—
    http://www.teach-nology.com/web_tools/ 140
Web-based Bookmark Management. 12, 17
Web-based Learning Model 1
Web-based Learning: A Practical Guide 1, 60
WebPractest 64

WebPractest Exercise (Figure) 64
WebPractest—
    http://www.wm.edu/CAS/modlang/gasmit/
    webpractest/ 139
WebQuest Evaluation Form 107
WebQuest 6, 8, 9
What is Inspiration? 43
When Is The Use Of a Worksheet Appropriate? 82
Why Assess? 101
Why Use Inspiration? 33
Why Use Search Engines? 120
Why Use Worksheets? 81
Window Bar and Creating Linked
    Windows (Figure) 31
Windows Tiled in Opera Web Browser (Figure) 32
Without the Words Field (Figure)................ 131
Worksheet Generator 83
Worksheet Generator 83–84
Worksheet Generator (Figure) 83
Worksheet Generator—
    http://school.discovery.com/teachingtools/
    worksheetgenerator/index.html.............. 140
Worksheet Wonders & More 81–100
Worksheets 9

Y

Yahoo 120

About the Authors

Mary Ploski Seamon is a native of Connecticut and now resides in South Carolina. She is the mother of two children—Trevor of Los Angeles, California and Socrates of San Jose, California. Mary is a former English teacher, assistant principal, and principal at D. W. Daniel High School in Clemson, South Carolina. She credits Dr. Jim Ray, superintendent of Spartanburg School District 3, for creating the vision of technology integration.

Eric J. Levitt is a native of Long Island. Eric and his wife, Carmen, make their home in South Carolina. They have a daughter, Grace. Eric taught high school social studies in Grapevine, Texas. For the past five years, he has been the technology trainer for Spartanburg School District 3.

www.ingramcontent.com/pod-product-compliance
Lightning Source LLC
Chambersburg PA
CBHW081155290426
44108CB00018B/2557